RHYTHMS OF CHANGE

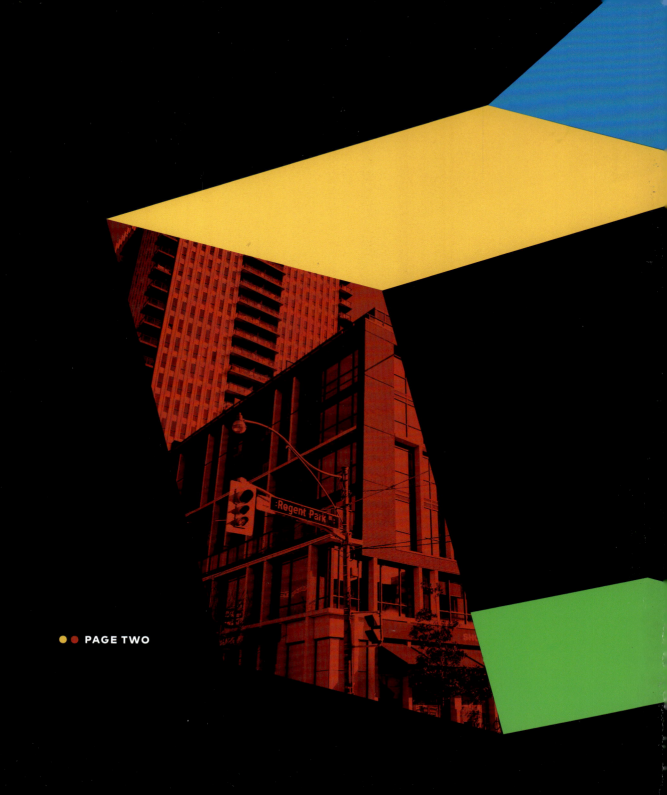

PAGE TWO

RHYTHMS OF CHANGE

Reflections on the
Regent Park Revitalization

MITCHELL COHE

CONTENTS

The Children's Book Bank *1*

Prelude *2*

SET ONE **TUNING UP** *7*

1 **An Unforgettable Moment** *9*

2 **But First ... The Back Beat** *12*
BRIDGE: Evolution of a Songwriter *16*

3 **From Montreal to the Land of Golden Opportunity** *18*

4 **To the Private Sector** *21*
BRIDGE: Another Life *25*
SOLO: John Daniels *27*

5 **The Garden City Story** *28*

6 **Roots of the Revitalization** *32*
BRIDGE: Principles of Revitalization *34*
SOLO: Derek Ballantyne *36*

7 **Seeds of Change** *38*

SET TWO **INITIAL MELODIES** *43*

    8   **First Encounters** *44*
           BRIDGE: FOCUS Youth Media Arts *46*
           SOLO: Martin Blake *49*

    9   **Into the Deep End** *50*

  10   **Getting to Know You: Health Services** *52*

  11   **Getting to Know You: A New Youth Centre** *57*
           BRIDGE: The GreenBox: A Place of Refuge and an Inspiration *61*
           SOLO: Trevlyn Kennedy *62*

  12   **Getting to Know You: Further Inspiration** *64*
           BRIDGE: A Simple Act of Kindness *65*
           BRIDGE: *Peter Pan* at Regent Park/Duke of York Public School *67*
           SOLO: Sureya Ibrahim *69*
           SOLO: Agazi Afewerki *70*

  13   **Taking a Step Back: Relocation Strategies** *72*

  14   **Four Early Decisions** *74*
           BRIDGE: Mi casa es su casa *79*
           BRIDGE: Demolition Day: February 6, 2006 *80*
           SONG: "My Piece of the City" from *The Journey Musical* *81*

SET THREE **INTO THE SWING** *83*

15 **A Rude Awakening** *84*
SOLO: John Fox *90*

16 **Continuity and Momentum** *93*

17 **Fishing for Commercial Partners** *97*

18 **Trauma, Sadness, Anger, Hope** *103*
BRIDGE: Show Love *106*
SONG: "Show Love" from *The Journey Musical* *107*

19 **Phase Two and Beyond** *108*
SOLO: Tom Dutton *110*

20 **Paintbox Bistro: More Than a Coffee Shop** *113*
SOLO: Lorraine Segato *114*
BRIDGE: "Don't Go Out Tonight" *118*
SONG: "Don't Go Out Tonight" from *The Journey Musical* *119*

21 **More Big Challenges: Internal Forces** *120*

22 **Fighting to Stay the Course** *124*

23 **On the Losing End** *129*

SET FOUR   **A CRESCENDO OF SOCIAL INFRASTRUCTURE** *135*

24   **Emerging Community Leaders** *136*
  SOLO: Deany Peters *137*
  SOLO: Ines Garcia *139*
  SOLO: Marlene DeGenova *141*
  DUET: Ibrahim and Ismail Afrah *142*
  SOLO: Gail Lynch *144*

25   **Primary Organizing Elements** *145*

26   **Food and Urban Agriculture** *149*
  BRIDGE: Friends of Regent Park *154*
  SOLO: Heela Omarkhail *157*

27   **The Shuter Manoeuvre: Active Sports and Recreation** *159*
  BRIDGE: Bones of Contention *164*

28   **Arts and Culture** *166*

29   **Showtime** *169*
  BRIDGE: Showtime: Take Two *170*
  SONG: "Dancing Down the Avenue" from *The Journey Musical* *171*

30   **Envisioning an Arts and Cultural Centre** *172*
  BRIDGE: Withstanding the Challenges of COVID-19 *177*

31   **Funding an Arts and Cultural Centre** *178*
  BRIDGE: Bringing Anchor Tenants to the New Cultural Centre *181*

SET FIVE **A FUSION OF MELODIES** *185*

32 *The Journey Musical* *187*

33 Memorable Moments from *The Journey Musical* *193*

34 A Balancing Act *196*
SOLO: A Tribute to Pam McConnell *200*
SONG: "From the Rooftops" from *The Journey Musical* *203*

35 An Evolution in Philanthropic Thinking *204*
BRIDGE: Creating a Social Infrastructure Investment Fund *208*

36 An Affordable and Accessible Community *210*

37 The Revelation of Social Procurement *217*
BRIDGE: "Quilt of Love" *220*
SONG: "Quilt of Love" from *The Journey Musical* *221*

38 Coming of Age: The World Urban Pavilion *222*

39 An Impactful Walkabout *225*

40 A Brilliant Outcome *228*

41 An Encore with Infinite Possibilities *230*

Outro *232*

Coda *236*

Liner Notes *246*

End Notes *250*

Photo Credits *251*

This book is dedicated with much love to:

*My parents, Sheila and Saul Cohen,
who taught me what it means to be a good person.
I wish you were here to share these moments.*

*My wife, Janice, the love of my life and my partner
in every aspect of our life together.*

The warm and welcoming reading corner within The Children's Book Bank at Daniels Spectrum.

THE CHILDREN'S BOOK BANK

I AM INSPIRED every time I walk into The Children's Book Bank at Daniels Spectrum in Regent Park. Kids browsing the shelves and choosing a book that will be theirs, not just to read but to keep... to own, adding to their personal bookshelf and ideally to a lifelong love of reading.

Since 2008, The Children's Book Bank has distributed 1.5 million books across Toronto with the goal of providing equal access to books for all children.

Today, literacy can't be taken for granted. It needs to be nurtured, and putting free books in the hands of young people is the most powerful way to improve literacy levels and socioeconomic outcomes.

Ten dollars from the sale of every print copy of this book in Canada will be donated to The Children's Book Bank in Regent Park.

Together, we can build a city and country in which literacy *can* be taken for granted. With that accomplished, anything and everything is possible.

PRELUDE

I AM INSPIRED to dream bigger every time I visit Regent Park.

And I am inspired to be relentless in pursuit of those dreams by every conversation I have with Mitchell Cohen.

And now, many of you will also be inspired by Mitchell Cohen and Regent Park. *Rhythms of Change* is a magnificent tour de force, reflecting personal experiences and those of so many comrades who brought the world's largest mixed-income social housing transformation to life.

I can't remember my first visit to Regent Park—sometime a decade ago or so. But I will never forget my first time meeting Mitchell: eight years ago, in February 2016. I had been invited to give a talk about mixed-income transformation as a part of an Ask a Professor series sponsored by a local community learning centre and Toronto Community Housing. After the talk, a tour had been arranged for my research team with Mitchell.

I had worked closely with many real estate developers by that point and had never met any like Mitchell.

His crackling energy and hipster appearance were more like a jazz musician than someone who dealt with political roadblocks, architectural renderings, engineering challenges, financial pro formas, and construction cost overruns most days of the week. His deep humanity and warmth were readily apparent, as well as his generosity of spirit and time. But most of all, there was a gleam in his eye and determination in his voice about the unique opportunity to achieve something unprecedented at Regent Park.

We strolled through the Regent Park buildings and landscape that afternoon, awestruck by what had already been achieved. My follow-up email to Mitchell sums up our reactions well.

February 8, 2016, 8:12 a.m.

Mitchell,
We will be savouring our visit to Regent Park for a long time. Truly inspiring for our team to see the parts of the vision that have already been accomplished along with your team's commitment to stay tenacious to achieve the full vision.

Thanks again for the materials. It resonates so much to see you write: "It was clear from the outset, however, that the real measure of success would not be the quality of the new homes, but rather whether an inclusive social fabric could be woven in which tenants and owners feel at home with each other and in their community, sharing the physical, cultural, and economic benefits generated by the revitalization." As you heard in my talk, we could not agree more.

Perhaps the best part of our visit was to hear your team, TCH staff, and resident leaders talk to us afterward about the validation that they felt, both at how special their achievements are, in the context of the broader field of mixed-income development, and how the ideas that they have for strengthening the work are well in line with conclusions that we have reached as well.

Reading that email today, I realize that "the context of the broader field of mixed-income development" has not changed much in eight years, nor have our "conclusions."

Developers across North America have demonstrated that it is possible to physically transform former no-go high-poverty social housing complexes into vibrant mixed-income housing redevelopments.

However, those redevelopments often displace the majority of the low-income residents of colour who originally lived in those communities. And those original residents lucky enough to surmount the challenges of relocation to return to the new mixed-income community often suffer stigma and a loss of influence and sense of belonging.

In our book, *Integrating the Inner City: The Promise and Perils of Mixed-Income Public Housing Transformation*, my co-author Robert Chaskin and I called this outcome "incorporated exclusion." Furthermore, many low-income residents of the new mixed-income communities remain in tenuous economic circumstances rather than being able to use the socially mixed housing as a platform for upward mobility.

In this inspiring and funky mambo through the Regent Park journey, Mitchell takes readers behind the scenes of each stage of this massive revitalization and demonstrates that it is possible, and indeed imperative, that we seek *both* social and physical transformation from mixed-income redevelopment.

And as Mitchell emphatically argues, the social transformation is not just about programs and services: "A paradigm shift was essential . . . from simply delivering services to delivering pathways to empowerment, personal growth, and capacity building."

As he takes us down memory lane, Mitchell provides intricate details of the decisions made and numerous financial and operational innovations that made this comprehensive redevelopment effort possible.

Along the way, he introduces us with wonderful tenderness and admiration to the many visionary and courageous community and organizational leaders whose roles and willingness to be timely disrupters made vital contributions to the Regent Park achievement.

If only Mitchell could pull out one of his little bottles of Wite-Out and blot out the political and societal dysfunction that makes these transformations so much more complex than they already are.

The Regent Park quest for urban equity and inclusion is far from over, and the next generation of local change agents will have to engage deeply with a new lead developer to prioritize social impact alongside real estate development in the remaining two phases.

But oh, what a miraculous and stupendous transformation has been achieved at Regent Park. And thanks to this mesmerizing rendition of the odyssey thus far, there are abundant lessons, strategies, and champions to deploy here and anywhere community members, local government, and private developers are bold enough to dream big.

Mark L. Joseph, PhD
Founding director, National Initiative on Mixed-Income Communities
Leona Bevis and Marguerite Haynam Professor of Community Development
Jack, Joseph and Morton Mandel School of Applied Social Sciences
Case Western Reserve University

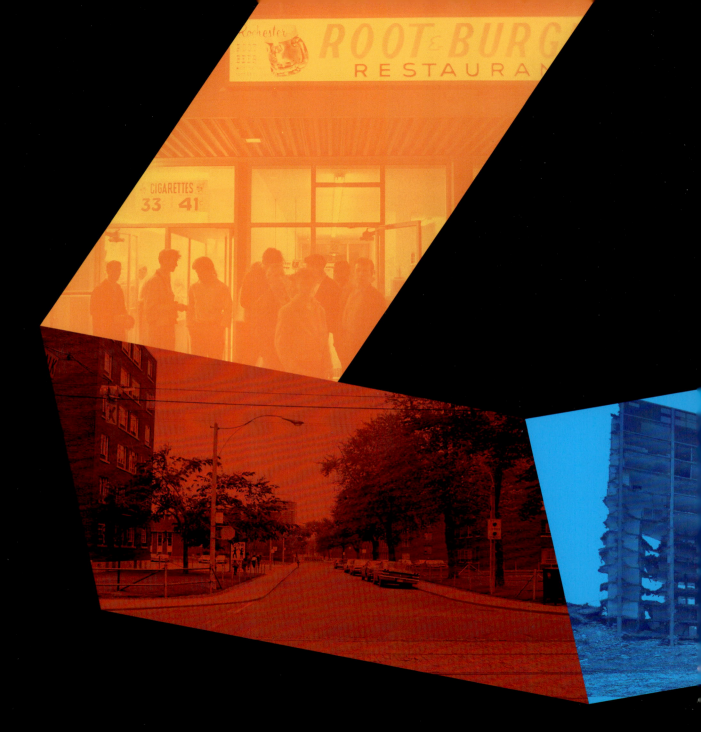

SET ONE
TUNING UP

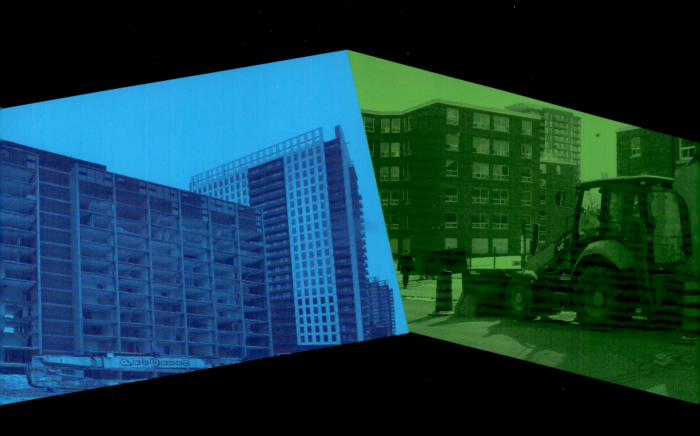

Demolition of 605 Whiteside Place, a fourteen-storey TCHC building in Regent Park designed by architect Peter Dickinson.

VERSE ONE

AN UNFORGETTABLE MOMENT

It was a cold but clear winter morning on February 6, 2006, the day demolition started. David Miller, mayor of Toronto, had overseen a process culminating in a truly historic moment in the life of the city, a moment both celebratory and heart-wrenching. That morning, Mayor Miller sat in the cab of a big machine near the corner of Dundas and Parliament Streets, pulling the levers that would tear a family's home apart.

Phase One of the Regent Park revitalization was officially underway.

As I watched the big rigs do their damage, one long-time resident, a grandmother, told me with tears in her eyes that her family and their history were being erased. Her words hit me like a wrecking ball. I felt the weight of responsibility to do right by the people who had lived in substandard conditions for decades, isolated from the outside world.

Toronto Community Housing (TCH) had promised residents a "right of return." But at that moment, it was just that: a promise, a hope that the authorities would be true to their word, and that residents would be able to come home to a new Regent Park.

Standing next to me were the true visionaries of the revitalization—Deany Peters, Diane MacLean, Debra Dineen, Neil Clarke, Ines Garcia,

Lloyd Pike, Sureya Ibrahim—and several hundred other residents, watching as their homes, memories, and lives were ripped apart.

In the middle of the tableau stood local councillor Pam McConnell, a lifelong crusader for social justice and steadfast champion of the revitalization. Pam's presence was powerful, reassuring her constituents that the promise of return was real.

From that moment, our team was part of a large ensemble, playing a pivotal role but always listening closely to the tones and melodies of the other players. There were moments when we had no idea where the music would take us. There were others in which the notes resonated in perfect harmony, reflecting hope, potential, and personal growth. Darker tones often took centre stage, reflecting anger, resentment, and a deep sadness for what had been lost.

We planted our feet in the centre of the process as the community was torn apart and actively participated in weaving it back together.

The entire city saw the remnants of lives on display as our demolition contractor exposed wires, steel, and the pastel colours of individual dreams, hopes, love, and family.

And then, ever so slowly, the city and the world beyond witnessed something special beginning to emerge. One brick at a time, building by building, block by block. Beautiful and messy. Important, imperfect, and the subject of great debate: *Is revitalization a genuine attempt at redevelopment that respects the people and history of a community . . . or is it simply gentrification in disguise?*

Academic research and kitchen table conversations will weigh that question for decades to come. And as the revitalization continues to unfold, films, videos, songs, and spoken-word poetry will chronicle personal stories, tragic and heroic, heartwarming and horrific.

    My reflections in this book flow from eighteen years of engagement, leading our team through the first three phases of the revitalization. I will play them out in five sets, with verses, solos, and bridges. The first three sets will shed light on the origins of the revitalization, as well as behind-the-scenes business and political stories. The final two sets reflect on social infrastructure and community development stories, with an emphasis on arts and cultural aspects of the journey.

    Although I am telling this story from my experiences and perspective, it is, above all, a story of remarkable people who recognized the need for change and then, through their will and determination, shaped what that change would be.

    This is their story, a story of resilience in the face of upheaval and transformation.

    It is also *our* story, the story of our company diving into the unknown, connecting and collaborating with local residents and TCH, our public-sector partner, hand in hand with an ensemble of players from beyond the community, each bringing the best of their love to the composition.

VERSE TWO

BUT FIRST...
THE BACK BEAT

I GREW UP IN REGINA and loved it there. Through the late '50s and early '60s, we were free to run the streets and back lanes, playing hard until well past dark. A couple thousand kilometres away, kids in Regent Park were likely doing the same, insulated within their "garden city" from the hustle and potential harm of the outside world.

My father was a local hero, a family doctor with a practice that specialized in treating alcoholism and drug addiction. Everyone loved Saul Cohen, and his black leather satchel was always by the front door, ready in case he had to deliver a baby in the middle of the night. Sheila, my mom, ran our household, welcoming our friends to her kitchen table and showering us with love, lunch, and her famous chocolate chip cookies.

I was the middle child, constantly chasing my big brother, Steve, who was always generous, letting me into football and hockey games with the big guys. My younger sister, Brenda, and I invented games that involved wild chases through the neighbourhood.

And there was music. We had a Heintzman piano, a gift from my *bubbi*. I made it to Grade 4 in Royal Conservatory training. Then one day, my teacher started whacking my hands with her ruler to correct my form, and I quit.

Those piano lessons, however, led to a lifetime of jamming, songwriting, and musical fun—which, decades later, would intersect with my work in Regent Park.

They were also a ticket to out-of-tune pianos at high school dances across the city. I played "keys" for Jay Walker and The Pedestrians, a rock and roll band fronted by Max Yuditsky, son of our Hebrew teacher and renowned for playing "Johnny B. Goode" better than Chuck Berry. Our most memorable gigs were Saturday nights in the summer of '67 at the only bar in Regina Beach. We'd be wailing away on "Louie Louie" or "Gloria" when, like clockwork, a slugfest would inevitably erupt on the dance floor between the locals and the cottagers. And we just kept playing that good old rock'n'roll.

And then, as young people with eyes to the future often do, I left home.

I applied to universities across the country—except, of course, the University of Saskatchewan. Too close to home. UBC, Carlton, Queen's, and U of T each offered a $500 scholarship, but McGill won me over, putting $1,000 on the table to seal the deal.

I couldn't fit a piano in my room at residence, so I bought a new Norman guitar. Lifelong friend and jamming partner Jerome Muller taught me the basic chords and progressions, and Danny Greenspoon's finger-picking style blew my socks off. Danny and I volunteered some of our free time at Drug Aid, an all-night crisis intervention line, talking people down from bad acid trips. Fortunately, most of our time was spent jamming.

After two years at McGill, it was time to travel even farther from home. Five pals and I crammed into a Volkswagen van in France and drove from Paris to Istanbul. We ditched the van in Istanbul and headed to Israel, Greece, Italy, and the ultra-hip island of Ibiza, where, wandering cobblestone streets among timeless stone buildings, I dreamed of becoming an artisan creating leather bags.

I woke up from the dream with an inventory of two soft leather briefcases and returned to McGill to complete a BSc in psychology in 1972, followed by a year at the London School of Economics, adding a master's degree in social psychology to my resumé.

Back in Montreal in July 1973, I made one of those casual decisions that magically establish the trajectory of one's life. I went to a birthday party of a friend of a friend of a friend. Hey, it was a party. Why not go? That night, I met and fell in love with Janice Lewis, and we've been making beautiful music ever since.

And then, with two university degrees and a serious girlfriend in the picture, it was time for me to get serious. I opened the Montreal *Gazette* and saw an ad: "Help Wanted: YMCA Community Worker—Social Work experience preferred, but not required."

It was perfect and led in a very straight line from there to here—the job that became a career and a life.

My office was a derelict basement apartment in a community of redbrick buildings known simply as "The Gardens." Reminiscent of growing up in Regina, kids from the Gardens would chase each other through the neighbourhood day and night, laughing wildly. In this neighbourhood, however, their parents, living on month-to-month leases, worried about the future.

They had good reason to worry. Wilful neglect by the landlord had the desired effect: the buildings would soon be beyond repair. And then, one day, the landlord issued eviction notices, giving tenants thirty days to leave the homes they'd been living in for years.

That day rocked my world. The vulnerability. The uncertainty. The precipitous ledge on which so many people live, striving to keep their feet on solid ground. And then one day the ground shifts, and there is no safety net to cushion the fall.

The contrast was stark. I had two university degrees, a steady job, and a family in Saskatchewan that could lend a financial hand if necessary. It was visceral... I had a responsibility to do something.

Sheila Rosenblatt and Sol Kasimer of the YMCA gave me the green light to push back, and together with local resident leaders Jeanie, Irene, and Harry, plus a large group of tenacious tenants, we pushed back with gusto. It began with three hundred tenants marching on city hall, not just to protest the eviction but also to propose a compelling alternative.

The secret sauce was a letter from Central Mortgage and Housing Corporation (now Canada Mortgage and Housing Corporation [CMHC]), offering $8,800 in "start-up funding" to assess the feasibility of buying or leasing the buildings under the governance structure of a non-profit housing co-operative.

City council listened carefully and refused to issue a demolition permit, leveraging an outcome that worked for everyone: we achieved a ninety-nine-year lease for half the site, and the landlord was allowed to build two buildings on the other half, rather than three on the entire site.

In 1976, three years after eviction notices were issued, the Gardens apartments became one of the first non-profit housing co-ops in Quebec.

A safety net was woven from a government housing program. It was win-win, and an early lesson on how to get things done. It also proved that if you present a compelling case, you *can* fight city hall.

BRIDGE
Evolution of a Songwriter

I've been a songwriter since my first girlfriend dumped me, shortly after I moved to London in September 1972. Nothing like an unexpected dumping to stimulate the creative juices.

Back in Montreal in 1973, I kept writing and started a record company, recording Stephen Barry Band Live at the Nelson Hotel in Old Montreal. The album sold a massive two thousand units, not quite enough to break even, but it sure was fun selling them from the trunk of my car on a "distribution" trip across Quebec and the Maritimes.

I also teamed up with Kevin Newton, Susan McCann, Donna Jacobs, Bryan Highbloom, and other pals to play R&B classics on the CEGEP and university circuit with a group called Esplanade.

A second awesome gig was playing jazz standards at the Wrong Number on Crescent Street with the Willis Knight Trio. Gordon Gibson played both bass and snare drum (yup... at the same time) while vocalist Donna Jacobs brought new life to the old standards. Decades later, Donna and I remain best friends and still play the classics when we get together.

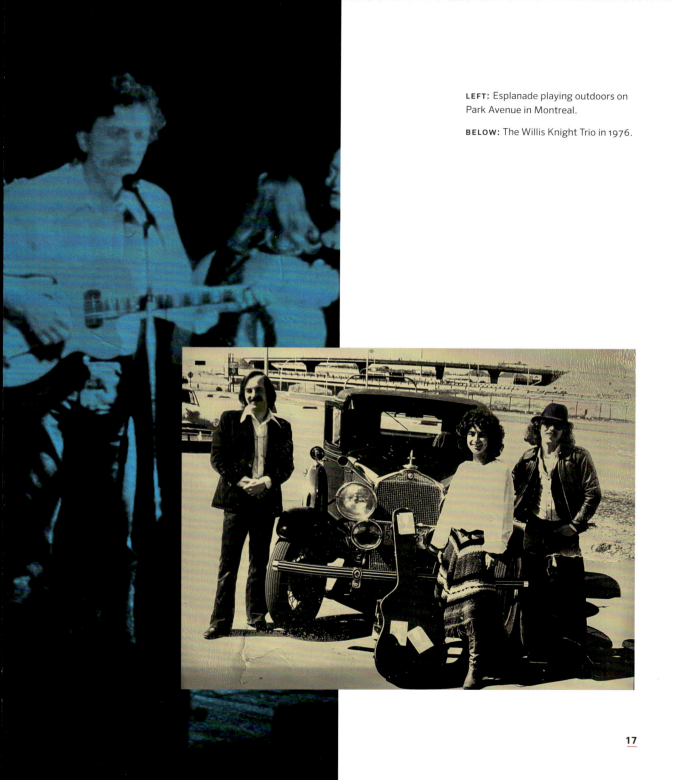

LEFT: Esplanade playing outdoors on Park Avenue in Montreal.

BELOW: The Willis Knight Trio in 1976.

17

VERSE THREE

FROM MONTREAL TO THE LAND OF GOLDEN OPPORTUNITY

Many of our anglophone friends left Montreal shortly after the Parti Québécois was elected in 1976. My jamming buddy Jerome Muller and best friends Peter and Judith Williams went "back to the land" in New Brunswick, which led to a short flirtation with the idea of building a future in Fredericton. Instead, in October 1979, we packed all of our worldly possessions into a small U-Haul and made our way to the land of golden opportunity: Toronto.

The cost of a decent apartment was a shocker: our seven-room flat at Durocher and Lajoie in Montreal had been a palace at $225 per month; now we were in a tiny two-bedroom apartment at Danforth and Greenwood Avenues in Toronto's East End, paying $450 per month.

Janice's nursing degree led to a job in adolescent psychiatry at the Hospital for Sick Children (SickKids). Not long after, I found a job for the ages with the Co-operative Housing Federation of Toronto (CHFT), a hotbed of activism focussed on affordable housing. At the time, the federal government was committed to a national housing strategy, investing in deep and long-term affordability with an emphasis on local capacity building and self-governance through the co-op housing model.

CHFT headquarters were in a rundown industrial building on the other side of town. My route to work took me through the notorious Regent Park, which generated a heads-up from friends that if I drove along Dundas Street, I should roll up the windows, lock the doors, and *not* stop until I came out the other side.

I was immediately inspired by the visionaries of the co-op movement. Mark Goldblatt, Alexandra Wilson, Jean Stevenson, Noreen Dunphy, Robin Campbell, Dale Reagan, Tom Clement, Bruce Woodrow, Marianne Moershel, and Diane Saibil welcomed a twenty-eight-year-old newbie to Toronto's affordable housing scene.

In a brilliant turn of foreshadowing, I met Pam McConnell shortly after I was hired. Pam was the chair of CHFT's board of directors, and I was incredibly fortunate to be in the nosebleed seats as Pam chaired the organization's annual general meeting in 1980. Pam was awe-inspiring as she elevated the entire room with her vision for the co-op housing sector.

My initial work at CHFT was nurturing board members for the Neilson Creek Housing Co-op in eastern Scarborough. Within a few months, Alexandra Wilson, unofficial leader of an organization without an organizational structure, convinced Mark Goldblatt to include me on his development team. A minute or three later, I was handed responsibility for buying land and negotiating construction contracts with developers and builders.

Interest rates at that time were on their way to a high of 22 percent, and even deep-pocketed developers took us seriously. With the clock ticking on high-interest loans, the development community came to us, not because they wanted to, but because they had to. There was no condo market, and rental economics made zero sense with interest rates in the high double digits and beyond.

This was a "seize the moment" opportunity for the co-op sector.

Although I knew zip about buying land and even less about construction, the team at CHFT delivered a brilliant mentor in Bruce Lewis, the co-op sector's go-to lawyer. Bruce and his partner, Nancy Collyer of Lewis & Collyer, understood everything about everything and were extremely patient in guiding me through the weeds and fine print.

I dove into those weeds with enthusiasm and took great pleasure holding feet to the fire, ensuring every aspect of contractual fine print was delivered. I was far from popular within the development community, but each new housing co-op incorporated every ounce of value we had negotiated.

Most importantly, those homes remain affordable today by virtue of long-term government investment.

VERSE FOUR

TO THE PRIVATE SECTOR

PAUSE FOR A SECOND and imagine the time between 1973 and 1984... an era in which our federal government acted on the belief that a secure and affordable home for all Canadians was the essential building block of a healthy society.

When the federal Liberals were defeated in 1984, Brian Mulroney's Conservative government began the slow and painful process of reducing federal spending on new non-profit rental communities. The government defended its spending constraints on constitutional grounds, stating that housing was exclusively a provincial/territorial responsibility. The Mulroney government eventually terminated all funding for social housing in its April 1993 budget.

The initial change of government and turn of policy in 1984 led to a monumental personal decision for me—that is, crossing the aisle to the private sector, joining John Daniels at The Daniels Group in April 1984. Some colleagues saw the move as a classic sellout. I saw it as an opportunity to create affordable housing from the platform of a private sector business.

Fortunately, it didn't take long to do just that. In Ontario, David Peterson's Liberal government took up the cause in 1985, opening the door for a young and aggressive team at Daniels to dive in with all feet.

Subsequently, in 1990, Bob Rae's NDP government expanded investment in affordable housing. In total, the Ontario government funded thirty thousand affordable homes between 1986 and June 1995, a testament to what can be achieved when political will is focussed and at least one level of government goes all-in on affordable housing.

Over those years, Tom Dutton, Mark Guslits, Jim Aird, Sam Tassone, and our team at Daniels developed 3,600 affordable homes in partnership with co-op, municipal, and private non-profit housing groups. Dutton and Tassone were a formidable team, developing disciplined design and construction methodologies that have been the foundation for everything we've developed and built over the ensuing decades.

Our approach was straightforward: co-design communities with non-profit stakeholder groups, provide a fixed price "turnkey contract," and deliver the goods for that price and not a penny more. The formula worked, and word spread quickly that we were doing this because we wanted to, not because we had to. Word also spread that we consistently outperformed expectations.

And then the government changed.

Our team at Daniels had an additional eight hundred affordable homes in the oven in June 1995. Those homes, along with seventeen thousand others in the pipeline, were toast the morning after Ontario's provincial election in June 1995.

Under the banner of a "Common Sense Revolution," newly elected Ontario premier Mike Harris terminated all investment in affordable

housing—no transition, no phase-out period. It was simply over. The new provincial government believed that a market unfettered by government intervention would deliver homes for everyone. Magical thinking at best. In fact, over the past three decades, we've witnessed the opposite.

The federal and provincial/territorial governments woke up briefly in 2002 and agreed to modestly invest in affordable housing. Subsequently, in 2017, the federal government launched a National Housing Strategy—but the damage was done.

Because of shifting political winds and "turn-on, turn-off" federal, provincial, and territorial housing policies and programs, there is no mystery as to why we are experiencing an affordability crisis today from coast to coast.

There are solutions readily available. Governments simply have to wake up and remember our history of housing successes and commit to investing deeply and consistently in a brighter housing future for Canadians.

BRIDGE
Another Life

I filled three binders with hand-scribbled songs that year at the London School of Economics, and several more in Montreal between 1973 and 1979.

In Toronto, I kept writing and teamed up with Richard Arfin and Manteca co-founder and music director Henry Heillig to create Another Life, a ten-piece R&B band. In addition to co-writing songs for the band with Arfin and Heillig, I acted as manager and promoter and landed a gig opening for Aretha Franklin at the O'Keefe Centre in May 1995.

Aretha had a bad cold that night and was in a mood to match. On the other hand, Another Life, fronted by vocalists Liz Tansey and Randall Kempf, rocked the casbah.

I was thoroughly enjoying my "other life" until the Common Sense Revolution forced me to put the band to sleep. The loss of our entire affordable housing portfolio required all creative and entrepreneurial juices flowing to the business rather than the band.

I did, however, continue writing and playing with Henry and donating songs to charities, including "Many Hands" for Habitat for Humanity and "Sisters" for the Sisters of St. Joseph.

We also wrote, recorded, and donated a song to the Regent Park School of Music. At the time, it was a one-off, but subsequently "My Piece of the City" became the centrepiece of *The Journey Musical*, which I'll tell you about in Set Five.

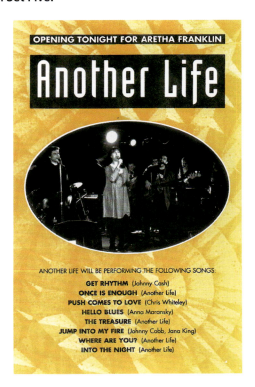

SOLO

JOHN DANIELS

I was young—thirty-three, idealistic, and with zero private sector experience. John Daniels (aka "Jack") was fifty-seven and a legend in the real estate industry.

I had helped create non-profit co-ops in Montreal and Toronto. Jack had built thousands of residential units in partnership with Eph (Ephraim) Diamond, Jack Kamin, and Joseph Berman at Cadillac Development Corporation.

When Cadillac merged with the Fairview Corporation in 1974, Jack spearheaded expansion across Canada and the US, helping Cadillac Fairview Development Corporation (CF) grow into the largest publicly traded real estate company in North America.

High interest rates that were a boon to the co-op sector in the early '80s were a challenge to developers across the country. Cadillac Fairview initially decided to sell its portfolio of twenty thousand rental apartments. It was the end of the road for Jack, however, when CF decided to sell its land division, including the 4,700-acre Erin Mills land assembly, the largest planned community in North America.

Recognizing the opportunity of a lifetime, Jack left Cadillac Fairview and bought the Erin Mills assembly in 1983 in partnership with Rudy Bratty, Fred DeGasperis, Larry Robbins, Marco Muzzo, and Elly and Norm Reisman.

The timing was serendipity: I was looking for a developer willing to put resources into creating affordable housing. And Jack was looking for someone to grow a company that would build on land in Erin Mills. Despite our differences in age and experience, we shared a passion for building community... and it was pure magic for thirty-eight years.

Over those years, we grew a company of three into a company of 450, creating forty thousand homes for people of all ages and incomes, successfully integrating affordable housing within our business strategy every step along the way.

VERSE FIVE

THE GARDEN CITY STORY

T HOSE RED-BRICK BUILDINGS at the Gardens in Montreal were the same vintage as many others built by the federal government after World War II. Some neighbourhoods, like the Gardens, were built to house veterans returning from the war, and others were chosen to renew areas of abject poverty.

One of those renewal neighbourhoods was Cabbagetown South in Toronto's Downtown East, home to Irish immigrants who had fled the potato famine of the mid-1850s. And yes, cabbages were literally grown in front yards throughout the neighbourhood. There were no sewers or sidewalks, and by the mid-1940s, most of the homes, built a century earlier, were beyond repair.

With the best of intentions, the federal government and City of Toronto envisioned Regent Park, a new form of public housing that embraced "garden city" planning principles. Initially envisioned by British town planner Ebenezer Howard at the end of the nineteenth century, a garden city blends the benefits of quiet rural living and an urban environment, hypothetically manifesting the best of both worlds.

With 2,083 units on sixty-nine acres, Regent Park was one of the largest experiments in garden city planning in the country. Although a short walk from downtown Toronto, it was light years away in all other respects.

Application of garden city principles in Regent Park was based on a simple premise: if you eliminated cars by removing public streets, kids would be able to play safely within the gardens. Open spaces would be plentiful, and courtyard buildings would provide a quiet refuge from the harsh realities of urban life.

That was the theory. On the ground, the reality proved to be quite different: cut off from the rest of the city and allowed to deteriorate by successive levels of government, Regent Park became an island unto itself, isolated and deeply stigmatized throughout the city.

Regent Park was built in two phases. By the early 1960s, construction of both North and South Regent Park was complete, and almost immediately, the community began to evolve demographically.

At first, a handful of folks made their way from the Caribbean to a new life in Canada, establishing a foothold in Regent Park. But it didn't take long before aunties, uncles, friends, and families followed, and within a few years, the food, music, and cultural gatherings throughout the community were infused with Caribbean fun and flavour.

Rhythms of change pulsed through the community over the following decades, with Regent Park becoming home to successive waves of immigration, from Vietnam and Cambodia in the '70s, Somalia in the '80s, and Bangladesh and South America in the '90s.

Although a strong spirit of community flourished within the garden city, the design itself created barriers between Regent Park and the rest of the world. Inward-looking and progressively deteriorating, the community was increasingly stigmatized.

For decades leading up to the revitalization, the media buzzed with coverage of guns, gangs, and violence. In fact, gun violence anywhere in Toronto's Downtown East was often characterized as taking place in Regent Park.

The result was a narrative that stirred fear throughout the city. For most Torontonians, that "roll up the windows, lock the doors, and don't stop" mantra I'd heard from friends was deeply established.

Aerial photo of North Regent Park prior to revitalization. The small park in the centre of the community was surrounded by buildings, invisible from Dundas Street.

VERSE SIX

ROOTS OF THE REVITALIZATION

IN THE EARLY 2000s, the Harris government took its Common Sense Revolution a step further, downloading responsibility for existing affordable housing to municipalities without the financial tools to retrofit and maintain homes in desperate need of repair.

Toronto inherited 58,000 homes, the vast majority of which had been allowed to deteriorate for decades. It was a nightmare scenario— the second-largest social housing portfolio in North America, downloaded by the province along with a repair backlog that quickly grew to over three billion dollars.

The City of Toronto responded by establishing TCH, a wholly owned subsidiary that would own and manage the portfolio. TCH's inaugural CEO, Derek Ballantyne, recruited from Ottawa's housing corporation, quickly recognized that the new housing company would need to be much more than a property manager: TCH would have to become a developer.

With that in mind, Ballantyne recruited Mark Guslits as chief development officer and member of the executive team. Guslits was a seasoned non-profit housing developer. While I was at CHFT in the early '80s,

Guslits was at Lantana Non-Profit Homes developing affordable communities in the St. Lawrence neighbourhood and across the city.

Subsequently, I invited Guslits to lead our affordable housing initiatives a few years into my tenure at Daniels.

After Premier Harris terminated the provincial program in 1995, Guslits went on to take charge of "Let's Build," Toronto's affordable housing facilitator, and from there made the move to TCH.

The mandate at TCH was clear:

1. Identify opportunities to substantially increase density in neighbourhoods across the portfolio.

2. Create value through intensification.

3. Leverage that value by engaging the private sector to create mixed-use, mixed-income neighbourhoods through *revitalization*.

In assessing how to kick-start the process, Ballantyne and Guslits applied the three primary rules of real estate investment: location, location, location. With those rules top of mind, it didn't take long for Regent Park, a low-density neighbourhood within walking distance of downtown, to rise to the top of the agenda.

Although location was a key factor, equally important was that Regent Park residents had engaged in deep discussions about the future of their community for close to ten years. That history of activism was critical, dating back to the early 1990s, when the North Regent Park Steering Committee pushed the provincial government to do something—anything—about deteriorating living conditions.

BRIDGE
Principles of Revitalization

The following is an excerpt from the Regent Park Social Development Plan:

Regent Park residents and agencies, with the City of Toronto and Toronto Community Housing, developed Community Planning Principles to measure the progress of the revitalization. The Principles were developed through an extensive community consultation process and have been accepted as the fundamental objectives of the Regent Park revitalization. The Community Planning Principles refer to both the physical redevelopment of the community as well as its social development.

- Renew the Regent Park neighbourhood
- Re-introduce pedestrian friendly streets and park spaces
- Design a safe and accessible neighbourhood
- Involve the community in the process
- Build on cultural diversity, youth, skills, and energy
- Create a diverse neighbourhood with a mix of uses including a variety of housing, employment, institutions, and services
- Design a clean, healthy, and environmentally responsible neighbourhood
- Keep the same number of rent-geared-to-income (RGI) units
- Minimize disruption for residents during relocation
- Develop a financially responsible strategy
- Create a successful Toronto neighbourhood
- Improve the remaining portion of Regent Park during redevelopment

At that time, the province was only willing to entertain a planning exercise on one small quadrant at the corner of Gerrard and River. Although this "think small" approach failed to launch, the unintended consequences have resonated through the decades. In short, that initiative brought residents together with urban activists, including former Toronto mayor John Sewell. Everyone shouted "hell no" to a piecemeal approach, leading to hundreds of meetings in kitchens and church basements throughout the community.

Emerging from that work was the all-important "right of return," a contractual guarantee that tenants would be welcomed back to a new home within their community. This commitment became a fundamental building block for everything that followed.

Hand in hand with the "right of return" was the agreement that tenants would continue paying rent geared to income and that their new home would be "right-sized" to reflect family composition. In other words, a family moving out of a five-bedroom townhome would be able to move into a new five-bedroom townhome if their family size remained the same.

Overall, the result was a set of principles under which a comprehensive revitalization could work for everyone.

SOLO

DEREK BALLANTYNE

Derek Ballantyne was an inspired choice to lead Toronto's new housing company. He was a dedicated public servant with an entrepreneurial spirit and a big-picture thinker who kept his eyes on every detail.

Derek was as comfortable promoting TCH's agenda in front of city council as he was around the kitchen table in a resident's home. In fact, he was often at kitchen tables throughout Regent Park, building relationships and trust.

In those discussions, Derek came to understand "right of return" as a fundamental building block for success. He also learned that moving tenants to the other side of town would erode the trust he was working so hard to build.

With that in mind, Derek and then CFO Gordon Chu utilized TCH's revenue stream as security to raise municipal bonds, enabling three "off-site" buildings to be built near Regent Park.

This was a master stroke in municipal finance planning. The off-site buildings allowed kids to remain in their schools and parents to maintain their social, health, and religious networks. The municipal bonds also enabled TCH to kick-start construction of Phase One of the revitalization.

Unlike many of his successor CEOs, Derek was with us in person at the partnership table—a true working partner—willing to make critical business decisions in real time, without delaying the process by consulting "head office." Derek *was* head office.

Derek's presence made an enormous difference, allowing us to build momentum every step of the way. And when his team made decisions, he had their back, empowering Mark Guslits, John Fox, Liz Root, Lizette Zuniga, Annely Zonena, Barry Thomas, and the entire team to push forward with confidence.

VERSE SEVEN

SEEDS OF CHANGE

A TRADITIONAL CONSULTATION is a one-way street: the public agency talks and the community listens. A box is checked... and the agency proceeds to do what they were planning to do well before the "consultation." Derek Ballantyne insisted on a consultation process that went far beyond the norm. Local voices were critical from the outset.

Most importantly, Ballantyne not only planted the seeds but also nourished their growth by underwriting a deep-dive engagement and consultation process, contracting Sean Meagher of Public Interest Strategy & Communications to build a process from the ground up.

Meagher was keen to bring his associate Tony Boston to the project team, believing that Boston's roots in the community would be a valuable asset. At the outset, Boston said, "Thanks, but no thanks." Having advocated for tenant rights as a community worker at Dixon Hall, Boston was uncomfortable with the notion of working for the "landlord." But Meagher was persistent.

As he considered the opportunity, Boston sought advice from the Three Wise Women of Regent Park: Deany Peters, Diane MacLean, and

Debra Dineen. Hugely influential voices in the community, they often held court on a bench in front of Root & Burger, the only place to buy a burger or anything else in Regent Park.

"May I approach the bench?" Boston asked respectfully and with a twinkle in his eye.

Dineen, MacLean, and Peters knew Tony Boston and trusted him. Their response was simple: *if* TCH was finally getting on with a revitalization and *if* they were going to send someone to consult with them, it should be Tony Boston—someone they knew and trusted.

In the end, Boston said yes.

Meagher and Boston's engagement work took place between July and December 2002, described in the executive summary of their report as follows:

> Hiring from within the major ethnocultural and demographic communities, TCH and their consultants built a team that could successfully engage residents. The project was rooted in the residents, who were employed as community animators, and who participated in every aspect of the project from process design to materials development. Relationships among residents augmented existing networks, to optimize dissemination of information and the gathering of feedback. This inclusive model won the trust of Regent Park residents.

Each sub-community within the community created a process that suited their sensibility. For example, Bengali men met in living rooms, while the women met outside in a circle, sharing opinions and feedback, with kids playing in the centre of the circle.

The process included intimate sessions led by local community animators, as well as larger meetings featuring "whisper translation" in seven languages, an acknowledgement of cultural and communication barriers within a community in which seventy languages were spoken.

Many old-timers were skeptical that government would deliver on their lofty promises. Lived experience with "government as landlord" provided little reason for optimism. Over the years, most residents had participated in many discussions about "change" and had experienced failed attempts first-hand.

This time, however, it felt different. The juggernaut of change appeared to be happening whether they liked it or not, leading to a very practical conclusion: it was best to raise their voices rather than sit it out on the sidelines.

In addition to the consultation with residents, TCH also sought input from urbanists and planners, including Ken Greenberg, Ronji Borooah, and John Gladki, as well as a host of architects, landscape architects, engineers, and economists.

Greenberg brought the sensibilities of renowned urbanist Jane Jacobs to the process, as well as expertise from his urban design work around the world. In addition to playing a pivotal role developing the neighbourhood plan, Greenberg engaged deeply in dialogue with residents, feeding concerns and interests back to the design table.

Gladki spent considerable time pounding the pavement in surrounding communities, meeting with the Cabbagetown Residents Association, Cabbagetown BIA, Cabbagetown South Residents' Association, Corktown Residents Association, and the Trefann Court Residents Association.

Some groups were very skeptical. Others welcomed the revitalization as a way to lift up the broader neighbourhood.

George Smitherman, at the time an Opposition Member of Provincial Parliament, was all-in on the revitalization and expressed strong support within Regent Park and his broader constituency, often directly confronting prejudices expressed by some neighbours.

The long, slow, and hard work of community consultation paid off. In February 2005, city council adopted a zoning bylaw that more than doubled the density over the sixty-nine-acre community, paving the way for the physical transformation. Remarkably, only one objection was filed with the Ontario Municipal Board, which was settled in advance of the hearing.

Equally important, however, was envisioning the evolution of a healthy social infrastructure. That work was brilliantly orchestrated by Chris Brillinger and his team at city hall, hand in hand with TCH and a large group of highly engaged Regent Park residents.

The outcome was the Regent Park Social Development Plan (SDP), a road map for the creation of an inclusive, complete community. This groundbreaking document incorporated seventy-five recommendations intended to guide the development of a healthy social infrastructure.

SET TWO
INITIAL MELODIES

VERSE EIGHT

FIRST ENCOUNTERS

As THE SEEDS OF CHANGE were taking root, I continued my daily non-stop drive through Regent Park on my way to and from work. In the early days, that route took me to CHFT's headquarters on Queen West, and subsequently to Daniels' head office at Queen and Yonge.

And then, in early 2005, with zoning in place and buildings deteriorating by the day, TCH was ready to act, first with a request for qualifications (RFQ) and then with a request for proposal (RFP) for the Regent Park revitalization.

With thousands of homes under our belt, including a wide spectrum of affordable housing under various government programs, we were qualified and deeply motivated to take on this monumental challenge. Along with four other developers, we made it to the short list and were invited to respond to the RFP.

After years of simply driving through, it was time for me to get out of the car, walk the courtyards within the "garden city," meet local residents, and listen deeply to the rhythms of the community. As we prepared our response, Martin Blake and I spent considerable time in the neighbourhood, listening and learning from local residents.

One spring evening in May 2005, I was hanging out with Deany, Diane, and Debra, along with Adonis Huggins, the executive director of Regent Park Focus Media Arts Centre (FOCUS).

Deany, Diane, Debra, and Adonis were sharing their dreams of what a revitalized Regent Park might look and feel like, and I was sharing my history in the co-op housing sector. And then I heard sirens coming.

I looked up and saw three police cars, lights flashing and sirens blaring, jump the curb on Dundas Street in hot pursuit of a group of teenagers hightailing it across a dusty baseball diamond. It didn't seem to matter that the high-speed chase could have ended in collateral damage to kids playing nearby.

This was my introduction to the community.

On reflection, the most surprising aspect of the experience was that no one was surprised. That moment spoke volumes about life in Regent Park, a reality that Deany, Diane, Debra, Adonis, and many others had been working hard to change for over a decade.

From left: Mitchell Cohen with Debra Dineen, Diane MacLean, and Deany Peters.

BRIDGE
FOCUS Youth Media Arts

FOCUS began its work in 1993 in response to concerns that Regent Park was unfairly stigmatized in mainstream media. Adonis Huggins and the FOCUS team had transformed an abandoned boxing centre in the basement of a TCH building into a media production hub.

I loved that basement space. At 4,500 square feet, it was seemingly endless and gritty to the max, a rabbit warren of rooms leading to other rooms, with young people of different ages populating all the spaces, playing drums in one room, recording audio for a broadcast on Ryerson's (now Toronto Metropolitan University) radio station in another, and in yet another, laying out copy and artwork for the next edition of *Catch da Flava*, a magazine with content written and curated by young program participants.

Every summer, FOCUS hosted a video production program for local young people, along with an annual community screening and celebration of their work, which would evolve as a forerunner of the Regent Park Film Festival.

In short, FOCUS was empowering young people to use video and media arts as a vehicle to tell the stories of their lives and community. Thirty-one years later, Adonis and FOCUS continue doing that important work.

Adonis Huggins inside FOCUS's Radio Regent recording studio.

SOLO

MARTIN BLAKE

Martin joined our team in 1996 and has led many business initiatives over the past twenty-eight years, including our twenty-plus-year partnership with Amica Senior Lifestyles. That relationship resulted in twelve new communities for older adults across the Greater Toronto Area (GTA), as well as an innovative "under one roof" approach that integrates a continuum of housing opportunities for older people, an approach that my mom thoroughly enjoyed over the last ten years of her life.

A passionate champion of affordable housing, Martin served as a board member and board chair for several terms at Habitat for Humanity GTA.

Martin's commitment to creating affordable homes, combined with his boundless energy and entrepreneurial spirit, resulted in groundbreaking shared equity mortgage programs that have been emulated by both provincial and federal governments.

Martin also put the puzzle pieces together with Sean Gadon of the City of Toronto to create our Partnership for Affordable Living (PAL) Program in collaboration with Sun Life Financial and WoodGreen Community Services. PAL is a highly replicable model integrating affordable rental homes within market rental buildings.

And when he had five minutes to spare, Martin spearheaded our partnership with the University of Toronto on a large student residence at Sussex and Spadina in downtown Toronto.

When the Regent Park opportunity appeared on our radar in 2005, Martin led our response to the RFP and has acted as partner in charge through every twist and turn on the journey. Like other senior executives, Martin truly is a *partner*, investing in every new Daniels community alongside Mr. Daniels and the rest of us.

Above all else, Martin is a brilliant mentor and teacher, ensuring that our next generation of leaders has the tools to take our company boldly into the future.

VERSE NINE

INTO THE DEEP END

TCH'S REQUEST FOR PROPOSAL clearly indicated a desire to sell market housing density to the highest bidder. Our time on the ground in the neighbourhood spoke volumes against that approach.

Our key takeaway was that a multi-phased sixty-nine-acre revitalization was a highly complex and textured process, with a myriad of competing interests and moving pieces. A decision relating to one small piece of the puzzle would impact how all the pieces came together... or failed to come together.

In short, we concluded that a partnership-based approach was the only way to go. The path to success required a public-sector partner with skin in the game over the long term, rather than one simply acting as a vendor selling density and not worrying about downstream outcomes.

Eyes wide open, we ignored the RFP guidelines and submitted an "Alternative Development Framework," a public/private partnership model in which risk and reward would be shared between the partners.

We also believed that once on the runway, it would be essential to maintain continuity and momentum to achieve lift off. A start-and-stop approach, with each phase tendered sequentially, would be the kiss of death. With continuity and momentum as fundamental building blocks, our framework incorporated a "Right of First Opportunity" to extend the partnership through to the end of Phase Two.

Having ignored 99 percent of the RFP response requirements, we weren't surprised when our proposal was rejected.

And then, the Universe surprised us: when negotiations with Cresford Developments, the winning bidder, went up in smoke, TCH moved quickly to issue a second proposal call. The second call was identical to the first in most respects but with a single paragraph on the last page that opened the door to an "Alternative Development Framework."

We marched directly through that door and entered into a public/private partnership agreement for Phase One that gave TCH the ability to extend the agreement to Phase Two without issuing a further RFP.

From that moment, we were all-in.

VERSE TEN

GETTING TO KNOW YOU: HEALTH SERVICES

ONCE WE were CHOSEN AS TCH's partner, the second stage of our "listen and learn" tour was to open channels of communication with social service agencies, most of which had been embedded in the neighbourhood for decades. These were important stakeholders, delivering health and social support services to local residents. Our goal was to build trust, ensuring each executive director felt comfortable enough to call us anytime, day or night, or to yell at us when we took a wrong turn.

At the same time, however, it was important to challenge each organization to move beyond its traditional service delivery model. "Same old, same old" just wouldn't cut it within the spirit of a revitalization. A paradigm shift was essential—from simply delivering services to creating pathways to empowerment, personal growth, and capacity building.

Having started my career within the social services sector, I was familiar with how agencies traditionally work within a scarcity framework, constantly competing for government dollars. The complexities of a revitalization demand that silos be replaced with a collaborative approach, from competition to collaboration and impact.

One of our first sessions was with Michael Blair of the Toronto Christian Resource Centre (CRC). Michael welcomed us with open arms and provided invaluable insight into the history of the community, including how Dundas Street marked a physical and emotional chasm between North and South Regent. Subsequently, Blair and his successor, Debra Dineen, introduced us to residents on both sides of the Great Divide, a hugely helpful vote of confidence by trusted community leaders.

We also spent considerable time with Greig Clark, chair of the CRC's board of directors and a passionate advocate of the revitalization. Clark, Dineen, and Blair recognized that the CRC could play a pivotal role, and their open arms set the stage for an impactful relationship with both the CRC and Fred Victor Mission, the CRC's successor organization. In fact, the CRC, in collaboration with the United Church of Canada, redeveloped its land into an important community hub, including eighty-seven units of deeply affordable homes.

In addition, Kevin Moore of CRC's Regent Park Community Ministry was an effective bridge-builder, bringing people of all faiths together to address the challenges of living through the physical and emotional disruption of a revitalization.

Our next significant session was with Sheila Braidek, executive director of the Regent Park Community Health Centre. Sheila was rightly worried about the impact the revitalization would have on the centre's ability to fulfill its core mission—delivering health care within a community in which seventy languages are spoken and in which a large percentage of residents are on social assistance.

Braidek was tough on us, making it abundantly clear that the Health Centre was struggling to keep up with demand. And now we would be bringing thousands of new people into the community, making it much more challenging for residents to access health care services.

I proposed a highly theoretical answer to that problem: let's bring more services to the community. Braidek and her team, however, had their hands full, with limited capacity to make a case to the government for additional funding.

The practical answer was that we had to take the lead.

It took time to get in the door, but I finally met Camille Orridge, gatekeeper of all funding within the Toronto Central Local Health Integration Network. Orridge, now a senior fellow at the Wellesley Institute, was the co-founder of Pathways to Education, and through that work had a special familiarity with and connection to Regent Park.

Orridge listened closely to my pitch with no expression on her face. Was she going to throw me out or embrace the mission? Finally, with a twinkle in her eye, she said something like, "This will be tough, but we can get it done." The first step in the process was to commission a primary care study. Although everyone could predict the outcome, the formal outcome was an essential ingredient on a pathway to funding.

It took a year and a half, but the study concluded the obvious: Regent Park's expanding population required the creation of a new primary care centre. With this tool in hand, I knocked on the door of former Ontario premier David Peterson, who introduced me to Minister of Health Deb Matthews. Minister Matthews asked Saäd Rafi, her deputy minister, to hear me out.

There were at least twenty civil servants around an enormous boardroom table at 777 Bay Street. My first observation on entering the room was that each participant had the primary care study in their hands or on the table. I took that as a good sign.

I sang and danced my way through the entire revitalization story... with perfect pitch. The performance landed squarely on the pivotal role the province needed to play within the revitalization: to ensure health care services were available for all residents.

Deputy Minister Rafi asked for comments from the table. At least seven team members responded that there was absolutely *no way* the Ministry could fund a new health centre in Regent Park. Disappointed but not surprised, I was packing up my dancing shoes when the deputy minister made a dramatic declaration, which went something like this: "We're doing this. Figure it out."

The overall process took seven years and a ton of heavy lifting, but Sheila Braidek's essential feedback led to a significant expansion in health care services. Today, the 27,000-square-foot Sumac Creek Health Centre, operated by St. Michael's Hospital, augments and complements the work of the Regent Park Community Health Centre.

A Dickinson building at Blevins Place in South Regent Park.

VERSE ELEVEN

GETTING TO KNOW YOU: A NEW YOUTH CENTRE

K ATE STARK, executive director of Dixon Hall, was enthusiastic from minute one about the potential benefits of the revitalization. When Martin Blake and I met Kate at her Sumach Street office, her response was crystal clear: This is happening. We can't go back, we can't stand still, we must move forward, so let's do it together. That meeting was a "hallelujah" moment for Martin and me. An important local stakeholder was willing to reimagine how her agency could make an impact in the community.

Top-line importance for Stark was the work that Sandra Costain and Kenneth Slater were doing with young people at the Dixon Hall youth centre, a two-storey unit at 44 Blevins Place, a TCH building slated for demolition in Phase Three.

I went to visit, and Slater welcomed me into the world of at-risk young men and women within their neighbourhood. Before sitting down to chat, Slater showed me a bulletin board covered with photographs of

RIGHT TOP: Kenneth Slater outside Daniels Spectrum.

RIGHT BOTTOM: The Bill Graham Youth Centre, Dixon Hall's new home for youth programming and its music school.

young men—along with news stories about their deaths. One by one, I heard stories of young men lost to gun violence.

As we stood at the bulletin board, kids came wandering into the centre and, after a few high fives and introductions, made their way to the second floor to hang out, safe within a space of their own. Slater looked at them as they disappeared up the stairs, turned to me, and said, "This bulletin board reminds us of the past. But it cannot be the future. Those kids are the future. They are why I'm here... for their future."

It was very clear that we couldn't just demolish 44 Blevins and hope for the best. We needed to put the puzzle pieces together for a new youth centre, which began by securing a piece of land in Phase Three.

Fortunately, Greg Spearn was in the CEO chair at TCH at the time, albeit in an acting capacity. Others would have said, "No way, leave it alone." Spearn enthusiastically said *yes* and instructed his team to prepare a land lease, setting the stage for one of the most important pieces of physical infrastructure in the community.

With land in hand, Kate Stark; her successor, Neil Hetherington; and board chair Rod Bolger moved forward with a capital campaign to realize the dream of a new home for the community's at-risk youth. Chaired by Bob Rae, with Vivien Dzau and Patrick Gossage as co-vice chairs, a determined team of civic leaders brought the corporate and philanthropic community to the table, topped off with a naming gift from Cathy Graham and the Honourable Bill Graham.

BRIDGE

The GreenBox: A Place of Refuge and an Inspiration

There were very few safe places for young people to hang out in the neighbourhood. Dixon Hall's youth centre was one. Another was to gather on top of green hydro boxes in the community... climbing above the noise and conflict of daily life into a zone of relative peace.

Moze Mossanen captured the importance of the hydro box as refuge in his 2016 documentary *My Piece of the City*. Keith Harradence attended the premiere at the Regent Park Film Festival and was inspired by the possibility of creating a next-generation version of the green box—a new place of refuge within the community.

Harradence brought Q&A Design to the table, with artists Pierre Quesnel and Coraline Allard envisioning a space that encapsulated a warm and loving embrace. Our team was inspired by Q&A's vision and integrated their GreenBox design into the "living lane" just north of Dundas between Sumach and River Streets, a vibrant urban place with four work/live spaces developed in collaboration with BlackNorth Initiative.

Artists Benny Bing, Melissa Falconer, Komi Olaf, and Morgan-Paige Melbourne bring life to this new lane in the heart of the city, and the GreenBox is both a reflection of the past and a new urban place for memories to be made.

Mossanen walked the streets of Regent Park and was inspired to make a movie. Harradence saw the movie and was inspired to act, and so it goes within a revitalization in which everything and everyone connects, and everyone can make an impact.

SOLO

TREVLYN KENNEDY

One of the young people I met that first day at 44 Blevins Place was Trevlyn Kennedy, a spoken-word artist who had found a creative home within the safety of the youth centre.

The second time I met Trevlyn was at a Dixon Hall event in a super-sized bank boardroom in the financial district. Kate Stark had brought the board, volunteers, and donors together to describe the evolution of their agency within the revitalization. I was there to meet Dixon Hall's loyal stakeholders and to socialize the fact that we would soon be demolishing the beloved but dilapidated youth centre. Our goal was that some of the people in the room would be inspired to support the ideation and creation of the next-gen youth centre.

Trevlyn had been invited to share an original poem describing her feelings about the transformation. The poetry was harsh and difficult to hear, but also moving and powerful. Trevlyn described the pain of disruption, of her world being torn apart, with shattered glass everywhere, reflecting shattered lives.

Shortly after that encounter, I invited Trevlyn to a conversation about a musical I had begun to envision. Mustafa Ahmed, Steve Harmony, and Trevlyn joined Heela Omarkhail and me in an honest conversation about the good, bad, and ugly of the revitalization, as well as the significant risks inherent in "outsiders" trying to tell the Regent Park story.

That conversation led to many others and ultimately to Trevlyn becoming a lead performer in every iteration of *The Journey Musical: A Living History of the Regent Park Revitalization.* Her powerful performance of "Don't Go Out Tonight" brings me and most of the audience to tears every single time.

Trevlyn, along with Luke Reece, currently associate artistic director at Soulpepper Theatre, also joined Heela and me as co-writers of a show in 2020. Reece, one of Canada's most decorated slam poets, was also set to direct. Unfortunately, the show was cancelled when COVID hit. Subsequently, Trevlyn co-wrote *Songs from The Journey* with us, a "greatest hits" version of *The Journey Musical*.

Trevlyn has inspired me since the moment we met. Today, she continues to make an impact as manager at Dixon Hall's Bill Graham Youth Centre. Trevlyn speaks the truth about her community with love and empathy, insight and kindness.

VERSE TWELVE

GETTING TO KNOW YOU: FURTHER INSPIRATION

Next stop on our "listen and learn" tour was with Alfred Jean-Baptiste, the executive director of the Toronto Centre of Learning & Development (CLD). Jean-Baptiste was there when we arrived in 2005 and is still making a positive impact today, an inspired collaborator throughout the process.

The CLD's contribution to the revitalization was super-charged when TCH offered the organization a highly visible storefront within Phase One. A physical presence is essential for building community, and CLD, with support from both the corporate and post-secondary institutional sectors, has been making the most of that opportunity ever since.

Our team provided seed capital for the first four years under the Daniels Centre for Learning banner. With proof of concept firmly demonstrated, Daniels and CLD brought TD Bank to the table as the "name on the door" sponsor, and the TD Centre of Learning has been projecting beautiful music into the community from the storefront ever since.

Over the years, Jean-Baptiste has brought many local residents to CLD's team, including Sureya Ibrahim and Agazi Afewerki.

Sureya, often referred to as the unofficial mayor of Regent Park, was instrumental in forming the Regent Park Catering Collective and Regent Park Sewing Studio, nurturing local caterers and seamsters. Afewerki's Youth Empowering Parents has grown from humble roots in Regent Park to a force for learning and empowerment around the world.

Partnership with community colleges and universities has been at the heart of CLD's work from the outset, an important demonstration of how cross-sectoral collaboration can bring value to all participants. For example, a long-term collaboration with the University of Toronto's

BRIDGE
A Simple Act of Kindness

Sandra Ryan of the Salvation Army was a particularly empathetic local leader, supporting clients through the challenges of isolation and poverty, challenges significantly exacerbated by the disruption of the revitalization process.

One memorable day, I was sitting alone in our Regent Park management office, contemplating the most recent roadblock that needed to be navigated. From out of the blue, Sandra dropped in, with no agenda other than to wish me well and share a particularly moving and relevant prayer from the Bible.

This was a beautiful act of kindness that refreshed my faith and refilled my energy tank.

Shauna Brail provided internship opportunities for students within Brail's urban studies program. In addition, Ask a Professor and a community advocacy program were initiated by Brail and the CLD team, bringing U of T faculty into the community to talk about their work.

These initiatives were a powerful demonstration of "communiversity," conceived by University of Toronto president Meric Gertler as a way to break down traditional barriers between institutions of higher education and folks on the ground in community.

CLD's groundbreaking work also includes a long-term collaboration between Ranee Lee of OCAD University and the Regent Park Sewing Studio. Lee, an entrepreneur, teacher, and innovator, developed DESIGNwith, a program that engages women from Regent Park in learning design for social innovation and the circular economy.

Our "listen and learn" travels also allowed us to build relationships with the leadership at Boys & Girls Clubs, the Salvation Army, Central Neighbourhood House, Yonge Street Mission, and Neighbourhood Legal Services.

The consistent message at each stop on our "listen and learn" tour was clear: We're here for the long term. Yes, we're going to build new sewers, roads, and buildings. But we're going to go beyond the bricks. We're here to build community.

BRIDGE
Peter Pan at Regent Park/Duke of York Public School

Local schools were also an important stop on our journey of discovery. Jason Kandankery, principal of Nelson Mandela Park Public School, became an active collaborator, and we also got to know both teachers and principals at Regent Park/Duke of York and Lord Dufferin Public Schools.

One such remarkable teacher was Neil Sorbie, who was producing a theatrical performance of *Peter Pan* with a stellar cast of kids in Grades 4, 5, and 6, including a young Mustafa Ahmed as Peter Pan. Today, Mustafa is a globally acclaimed artist. His charisma was already evident on that auditorium stage, and the show was remarkable.

Just as Captain Hook was trying to get Peter Pan to walk the plank, Derek Ballantyne, CEO of TCH, received a text and learned about a devastating fire, happening in real time... in a TCH building.

In that moment, I came to fully understand the challenge of managing a portfolio of 58,000 housing units, all of which had been allowed to deteriorate well beyond a state of good repair.

SOLO

SUREYA IBRAHIM

CLD's innovative Immigrant Women Integration Program (IWIP) was a powerful program helping local women develop leadership skills. As part of that program, Sureya Ibrahim and other women from the community made videos chronicling their personal journeys through the relocation and "right of return" processes. Sureya and her family were the last to move out of Phase One, temporarily relocating outside of Regent Park.

Sureya's video touched our hearts—deeply. In the final weeks before her move, there was only one light bulb working down a long dark hallway. Cockroaches had taken over the building, and the sounds of pipes groaning in the middle of the night were nightmarish, imprisoned voices reverberating through the darkness, bouncing off the walls of an empty building that had once been called home.

Sureya's video also captured the essence of the relocation and "right of return" concept. The City and TCH delivered on the promise, making the challenges of the past a distant memory. Most importantly, Sureya was proud of her new home and excited to invite friends and relatives for a visit.

Sureya is now the supervisor of community connections for CLD, and in that role, she opens doors and unleashes potential within countless Regent Park residents. Person by person, day by day, year by year, Sureya does the long, slow, and quiet work of building community.

SOLO

AGAZI AFEWERKI

Alfred Jean-Baptiste also invited Agazi Afewerki into CLD's orbit shortly after opening CLD's storefront office. Agazi was born in Germany in 1987 after his family escaped civil strife in Eritrea. Agazi and his family immigrated to Canada in 1991 and landed in Regent Park in 1995.

I met Agazi in 2011 and was inspired by his quiet wisdom and steadfast determination to turn the typical teaching/learning paradigm on its head. Not long before we met, Agazi and Mo Shafique, a pal from Lord Dufferin Junior and Senior Public School, had an idea that they eventually turned into a global movement.

The thesis was breathtakingly pure: young people become teachers. Adults and seniors become learners. Youth Empowering Parents (YEP) was born from that idea. Piloted with ten youth and ten adults in the summer of 2010, YEP won a United Nations Intercultural Innovation Award a year later, the youngest organization ever to receive the award.

Agazi continues to inspire me today, as he drives YEP's impact through more than eighty locations around the world. YEP is a veritable "micro-leadership" pipeline, empowering young people from diverse cultural backgrounds to view themselves as teachers.

VERSE THIRTEEN

TAKING A STEP BACK: RELOCATION STRATEGIES

IMPLEMENTING THE "right of return" principle is an enormously complex undertaking. The health and well-being of all residents are at stake. TCH tapped Public Interest Strategy & Communications a second time to consult residents on relocation strategies. Sean Meagher and Tony Boston brought in York University students who trained tenants on "community responsive polling," establishing a baseline of tenant preferences with respect to relocation, as well as a system by which choices would be offered when the time came to move.

One of those local displacement choices was to move permanently into a new off-site building within a few blocks of their current home. These local off-site buildings were critical to the process, allowing social, medical, educational, and religious connectivity to remain intact for tenants despite the requirement to move out of their homes.

Another local displacement choice was a temporary move into an off-site building and then back into Regent Park when new buildings were completed. A second two-move scenario would be to move into a building within the Regent footprint that would be demolished in a later phase.

Although not everyone was happy with the choices, the key was that they had *choice*, rather than an ultimatum. Most families in Phase One chose one of the three off-site buildings, and most moved back into Regent Park once new buildings had been built.

Most importantly, local displacement allowed all of the buildings in Phase One to be demolished and replaced within a very short period of time. Speed was an essential ingredient, demonstrating to tenants, prospective condo owners, and commercial tenants that the revitalization train was real and moving quickly.

Unfortunately, in later phases, the idea of local displacement was shelved in favour of "anywhere displacement."

There was no appetite for building additional off-site buildings close to Regent Park, which meant that the choices for Phase Two and Three tenants were to live in Scarborough, North York, or Etobicoke for years, completely disconnected from their lives and networks in Regent Park.

Anywhere displacement challenges are enormously disruptive but can be mitigated with an investment in social support services for tenants within their temporary neighbourhood. Sadly, for tenants going through the process, those investments were never made.

This was very rough for hundreds of households. The backlash from anywhere displacement was significant, and in subsequent revitalization initiatives, including Alexandra Park and Lawrence Heights, TCH chose a "zero displacement" strategy in which all tenants relocated within the footprint of their community.

Although this causes less disruption, zero displacement significantly extends both the timeline and cost of revitalization.

In the "lessons learned" department, local displacement is the way to go—balancing the practical reality and challenges of a revitalization with an idealized scenario in which an entire community is transformed without disruption.

VERSE FOURTEEN

FOUR EARLY DECISIONS

SEVERAL CRITICAL early decisions set the stage for what has unfolded over the past eighteen years.

As we were finalizing details of our public/private partnership, Mark Guslits invited us to a meeting at TCH headquarters. We weren't sure what to expect. Tom Dutton, Martin Blake, and I walked into the big boardroom and found at least twenty people, including Guslits, Derek Ballantyne, and other members of the TCH team, along with a large group of outside consultants.

It was clear they'd been at it for some time. Empty coffee cups were scattered across the enormous table, along with papers and file folders haphazardly covering almost every square inch of real estate. Blank marketing foam boards sat on easels, seemingly poised for a big reveal. The tension in the room was clearly discernable. We soon learned that discussions had been underway as to what the revitalized community should be called.

The gurus providing marketing advice were very clear: the name of the community must be changed. In their view, the stigma associated with Regent Park was too powerful to overcome, and prospective purchasers would run the other way if the community kept its name. To demonstrate how that thesis would be manifested, they had created logos and pretty pictures supporting a name change to either Cabbagetown South or South Cabbagetown.

    Fortunately, Guslits and Ballantyne wanted to hear from their new partner before a decision was made. This was a no-brainer. Our response was clear: changing the name was a non-starter. Regent Park was and would always be Regent Park. We needed to respect the past if we were going to help build a future.

    The second piece of advice from the consulting team was that we locate the sales centre outside the neighbourhood, perhaps near Dundas Square to facilitate subway access. To the outside consultants, this was less a recommendation than an indisputable necessity. The prediction was that a sales environment within the community would be vandalized and prospective purchasers would *not* venture into the community.

    We said *no way* to that as well and with TCH's support made the second critical decision: design and build a presentation centre facing directly onto Dundas Street within Phase One. It was essential to say, "Hello, we're here, and we're part of your community."

    Although there were a few tense moments at the boardroom table, we came away energized by an understanding that TCH was embracing the partnership model, welcoming our voice and recommendations.

    A third critical decision was to "stop the music" on the phasing plan. Sixty-nine acres in the heart of the city was an enormous piece of land and would need to be developed in phases. But despite the advice of planners, architects, urban designers, developers, and economists, the phasing plan was totally wrong. For example, the big public-facing park,

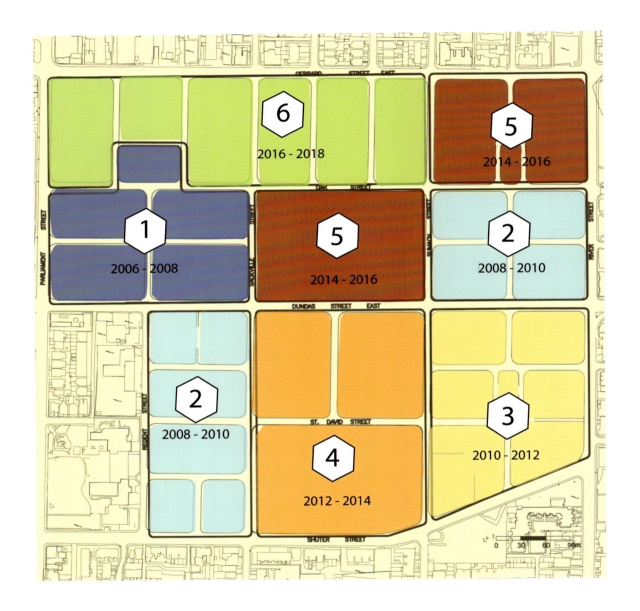

Initial phasing plan approved by city council in 2005. The park in the centre of the sixty-nine acres was planned for Phase 5.

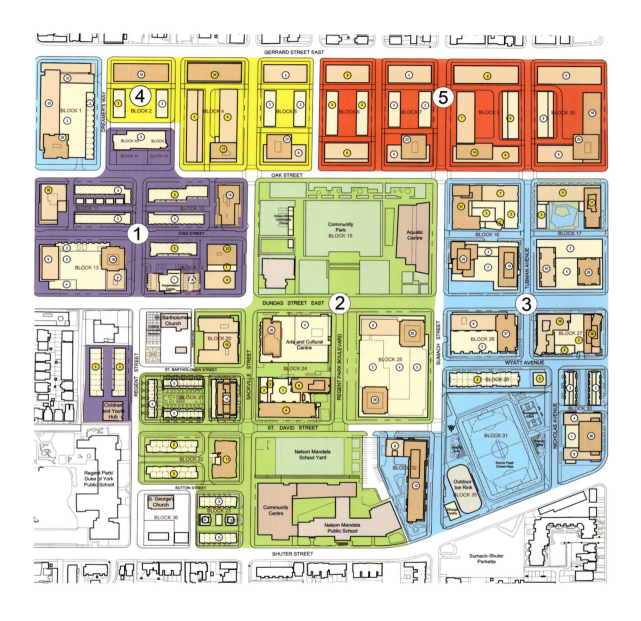

Revised phasing plan with the big park, Aquatic Centre, and Daniels Spectrum in Phase Two and the Athletic Grounds in Phase Three.

the centrepiece of the revitalization, had been relegated to Phase Five, at least fifteen years down the line. This had to be fixed or the entire project would be dead in the water. I pulled out the first of several bottles of Wite-Out that would be deployed over the course of the revitalization and drew a rational roll-out wherein one phase naturally flowed into the next, a stark contrast to the approved plan.

Guslits and the TCH team embraced our recommendation to shuffle the phasing deck, and Councillor McConnell shepherded a much-improved phasing plan through council, bringing the big park into Phase Two rather than Five.

At the same time, Councillor McConnell secured funding for an enormously important piece of physical infrastructure—a regional aquatic centre, now fittingly known as the Pam McConnell Aquatic Centre.

The fourth critical decision was to build our first market condominium without pre-sales—on spec. Generally, a developer will only be able to secure financing for a condominium with approximately 70 percent of the suites pre-sold.

We knew that would be a very tough sell. We also needed to demonstrate that the revitalization was real—that a mixed-income, mixed-use community was more than a pipe dream. With that in mind, we made the case to TCH, and our partnership agreed to build our first condominium without a single pre-sale.

All of these fundamental decisions paved the road to long-term success.

In the short term, we moved quickly to break ground on One Cole, our first condominium at Parliament and Dundas Streets, the western gateway into the community. Everyone was excited that construction was underway, that the long-promised revitalization was moving forward.

BRIDGE
Mi casa es su casa

Well before opening the Presentation Centre as a sales venue, we opened our arms to the community with lunch and dinner gatherings for Regent Park residents. The message was clear: the centre would be the community's as much as ours.

With that in mind, the communal space within the Presentation Centre was well used throughout those early years. FOCUS hosted a monthly open mic night called Last Fridays, featuring Da Youngstas or the Regent Park Divas, with local performers showcasing original songs and spoken-word poetry.

The Presentation Centre also hosted board meetings over many years for non-profit agencies in the community.

The Regent Park Presentation Centre located at Dundas Street East and Regent Street.

BRIDGE

Demolition Day: February 6, 2006

On the day demolition started, I returned home in the evening and, with echoes of that wrecking ball reverberating in my head, picked up my guitar and reflected on the impact of what we were doing... erasing so many memories. I also reflected on the resilience of residents who were able to mourn what they were losing while embracing the potential of what might be gained.

A few weeks later, co-writer and producer Henry Heillig took us into the Canterbury Music Company and the hands of Jeremy Darby, one of Canada's greatest recording engineers. Jackie Richardson and ten singers from the Regent Park School of Music recorded "My Piece of the City" that day, a song that became the centrepiece of *The Journey Musical*.

"MY PIECE OF THE CITY" from *The Journey Musical*

Buildings coming down, I hear the wrecking ball. Yes, they're coming down, we got the curtain call.
For the better they say, the Park must fall, for the future they say, it still hurts, that's all.

Maligned in the city, so misunderstood, it's my piece of the city, both bad and good.
I know it ain't pretty, but it's my neighbourhood, no it ain't pretty, it's my neighbourhood.

So many faces to remember, so many neighbours torn apart.
Childhood places gone forever, but always here, here in our hearts.

Buildings coming down, everything I've known.
And when we brought 'em down, I kept a brick of my own.
It's my piece of the city it's my home. It's my piece of the city, it's my home.

So many faces I remember, are coming back home to the Park.
Brand new places to discover, finding a new home, here in our hearts.

Well, we're movin' 'cross town, be back before long, to a new Regent Park, it's coming on strong,
A new piece of the city, a whole new song, a new home for the city, that's where I belong.

It's my piece of the city, it's my home, it's my piece of the city, got a brick of my own.

SET THREE
INTO THE SWING

VERSE FIFTEEN

A RUDE AWAKENING

AND THEN the world economic order disintegrated in October 2008. We were pouring concrete on the sixteenth floor of One Cole when *boom*, the world fell apart. It felt like another enormous wrecking ball. Although there were many sleepless nights, we had no choice but to keep pouring, fingers crossed that the tide would turn.

There had always been skeptics and naysayers, but the global economic meltdown brought many more out of the woodwork. For example, on October 4, 2008, a headline in the *Globe and Mail* declared "Condo Cash Was Going to Save Regent Park. Kiss That Idea (and Others) Goodbye." The article went on to say, "Barring a miracle, the new tower now rising at the corner of Dundas and Parliament will be the last evidence of the much-anticipated revitalization of Regent Park."

Waking up to that story in Canada's national newspaper was the ultimate definition of a "rude awakening."[1]

A month later, the situation went from bad to worse. Sobeys, our supermarket tenant, decided to walk away from a firm agreement to open a 27,000-square-foot store at the base of One Cole.

Initially, we had gone out to Canada's big three supermarket operators, shortly after being awarded the contract. Loblaws said it was interested and would be thrilled to put a 75,000-square-foot superstore in Phase One, as long as it could be surrounded by surface parking, a concept that wasn't a match for the vision. Metro showed promise but never came across with an offer to lease. And then along came Sobeys... ready, willing, and excited to add a store to its roster of Urban Fresh locations in Toronto. Our goal was to change the dial on how Regent Park was perceived within the broader city, as well as how residents viewed themselves within that context. The evolving community could not be just about the lowest possible price of housing and services.

With that in mind, we had been clear from the first conversation: we would not accept Sobeys' Price Chopper brand in the revitalized Regent Park. With that understanding between the parties, we had hard negotiated every aspect of a lease agreement, which included a requirement that the new store be branded as Sobeys.

And then the proverbial you-know-what hit the fan.

It started innocently enough. One of my colleagues received a call from an admin assistant at Sobeys asking for a meeting. My partner, Dominic Tompa, and I agreed to meet the Sobeys rep at our presentation centre. We were excited: perhaps they wanted to chat about our local hiring policies and how to kick-start the process. That would have been fun.

The Sobeys team sent a hard-nosed hatchet person to spill the beans. I made coffee for the three of us and we settled into folding chairs beside the big community model in the Presentation Centre. Dominic and I were looking forward to a creative conversation. Instead, the Sobeys

Concept drawing of One Cole with Sobeys branding, and the subsequent FreshCo by Sobeys.

spokesperson told us in four terse sentences that they were drop-kicking us through the goal posts. In short: Sobeys had made a big mistake. The fellow who had made the mistake had been fired. A Sobeys store in Regent Park would bleed red forever. And therefore they were splitting the scene.

And then he was gone. Never seen before, never since.

This was truly a "holy shit" moment. Catastrophic. Six months from launch day on a condominium with zero pre-sales, at a moment when banks and other businesses, large and small, were failing around the world.

For over a year, our marketing program had been featuring a rendering of One Cole with a prominent Sobeys banner anchoring the composition. More importantly, a grocery store was at the top of our Phase One deliverables, an essential ingredient to the overall revitalization.

We had to deliver a grocery store. However, despite a firm legal agreement, Sobeys was content to fight it out in court.

The tide turned at a pivotal meeting at Sobeys' Ontario head office. There were seven lawyers and senior executives on one side of yet another extraordinarily long boardroom table. On the other... John Fox, TCH's brilliant and doggedly determined in-house lawyer, and me.

With grim faces all around, the Sobeys team staked out their position, reiterating their spokesperson's mantra: "We're walking."

We staked out ours: "No, you're not."

It was clearly a standoff heading for the courts—until we deployed our secret weapon: John pushed Play on a recording from our groundbreaking celebration, at which a senior Sobeys executive waxed poetically about the company's long-term commitment to the community.

Obvious squirming on the other side of the table telegraphed that our secret weapon had touched a nerve.

Then came five months of tense negotiations, with many scary moments along the way. At first, an offer came forward that they would stick with all terms of the lease but with a Price Chopper store.

We said, "Hell, no. You promised Sobeys. We want Sobeys."

Tensions rose to the max as the clock ticked down toward our May 2009 sales launch, which was only a few months from first occupancies. Were we going to court? Or were we going to the market with the Sobeys store we'd been promised?

Two weeks before launch day, the Sobeys team presented FreshCo as an alternative. With the deadline looming, we shook hands on the new branding, but with a proviso that the store would be called "FreshCo by Sobeys" for the first ten years.

We'll never know whether it would have happened otherwise, but within a short time, eighty-eight Price Chopper stores across the country were rebranded as FreshCo. We did, however, take great satisfaction that forever and always, from one end of the country to the other, there would be only one FreshCo by Sobeys.

SOLO

JOHN FOX

Derek Ballantyne attracted the best and brightest to his leadership team. Transforming a portfolio of 58,000 social housing units was a worthwhile mission for people across all city-building disciplines.

John Fox became TCH's in-house general counsel in 2005 and represented the housing company as we negotiated our joint venture agreements for market condominiums and construction contracts for the delivery of TCH's replacement rent-geared-to-income (RGI) housing.

Creating agreements governing our public/private partnership was a deeply complex piece of work. Martin Blake led our side with wise and steady support from Brian Finer of Bratty & Partners.

John Fox was seriously tough and deeply committed to protecting the public interest. He was, however, also committed to finding solutions to complex problems, to charting a course to "yes" rather than taking the easy route to "no." John was a true champion for affordable housing, dedicated to the spirit of what we were going to do together. With John at the table, we found a path that worked for both sides, one that produced results that are celebrated around the world today.

For John, this was never about just the legal agreements. It was about people... and creating the underlying legal constructs within which the lives of TCH tenants would be significantly improved—not only with new homes, but also with new hope and ambition.

From left: Mayor David Miller, TCH Board Chair David Mitchell, Mitchell Cohen, Councillor Pam McConnell, MPP George Smitherman, and TCH CEO Derek Ballantyne celebrate the extension of the public/private partnership through all phases.

VERSE SIXTEEN

CONTINUITY AND MOMENTUM

As we worked through the Sobeys challenge, we were also deeply engaged in discussions with TCH about extending our partnership agreement to include all phases. Our thesis was clear: the pathway to success would be built on an ability to think and act on an *all phases* canvas. Success would be limited if we were constrained by the boundaries of Phase One, with only an "if/come" possibility that we would be engaged for Phase Two.

With that in mind, we made a strong case for continuity. We needed to tell a comprehensive story to prospective owners and their families, projecting confidence that pioneer purchasers wouldn't be hung out to dry, abandoned by a change in government policy or a stop-and-start tendering process that significantly delayed the transformation.

With momentum building toward the One Cole launch, Ballantyne, Guslits, Fox, and the TCH board embraced an all-phases amendment. On April 28, 2009, Toronto mayor David Miller and TCH announced a "Phase Two and Beyond" extension of our public/private partnership agreement.

This was another "hallelujah" moment. The "continuity and momentum" song we'd been singing had sunk in, embraced by both the City and the housing company. At that moment, TCH and the City committed to a long-term partnership, opening the door to making beautiful music together through all phases of the revitalization.

Over the long term, the impact of that commitment was momentous: without it there wouldn't have been an arts and cultural centre or health centre in Phase Two, or athletic grounds and Dixon Hall youth centre in Phase Three.

In the short term, we also had a much more compelling story to tell. And in the face of a global economic meltdown and dire predictions of doom and gloom, we needed a powerful story.

Millions of dollars had already been spent on spec in the hope that we'd be able to sell condominiums in Regent Park. More money was being spent every day as our "gateway" building took shape. If we didn't sell, it was over, and it would be a workout situation, discounting purchase prices simply to cover costs, let alone make a profit. In short, failure was not an option. So all hands were on deck to chart a path to success.

One of the tools was to sell suites to senior executives at both Daniels and TCH—at full price and only after the public was invited to choose suites at our launch events. Although this was a common practice at Daniels, in this instance, it was an essential ingredient. We were prepared to walk the talk, personally investing in the future of this community. Derek Ballantyne and a few others at TCH also put their money on the line, as did Councillor Pam McConnell, demonstrating a personal commitment to long-term success.

In addition, Martin Blake and Dominic Tompa worked hand in hand with TCH to create the Foundation Program, a powerful hand up to homeownership for TCH tenants. This program provided an interest- and payment-free "shared equity" second mortgage for up to 35 percent of the purchase price, enabling seventeen TCH tenants to become homeowners at One Cole.

Dominic and Martin also developed the BOOST Program, a further down payment assistance program offering interest- and payment-free second mortgages for up to 10 percent of the purchase price. This opportunity helped first-time buyers from across the city become homeowners within Regent Park.

Funding for both the Foundation and BOOST programs was sourced through collaboration between Daniels, TCH, and Sean Gadon of the City of Toronto's Affordable Housing Office (now called the Housing Secretariat), an expression of partnership and solidarity. We were in it together, shoulder to shoulder, finding solutions to the challenges du jour.

Daniels' CFO, Jim Aird, and our vice president of finance, Judy Lem, worked with Tompa and RBC to create an innovative gradual deposit plan. With only $3,000 required on signing a purchase agreement, and $1,000 per month to a maximum 5 percent down payment, the transition from tenant to homeowner became much easier.

Storytelling is an essential ingredient to any successful marketing campaign. Simona Annibale, vice president of marketing, and our colleague Heather Lloyd rose to this challenge. Bob Froese and Dorothy McMillan of creative agency Bob's Your Uncle (BYU) were brought on board along with Rhoda Eisenstadt, Carol King, and David Eisenstadt of the Communications Group. With their input and strategic advice, we built a powerful narrative about transformation and the opportunity for early adopters to help shape the future of the community.

Bottom line: we also needed a strong response from the real estate community. We could build a powerful story and deliver great prices, but without brokers and agents having faith in the future of the community, we would have fallen flat. Linda Thompson, Lamis Dantas, Dan Wong, Tony Ma, Dennis Liu, May Liu, Brady Gong, and a host of other real estate professionals became vocal champions of the revitalization.

The proof was in the proverbial pudding, with just under 60 percent of One Cole sold within a month of the opening. The naysayers would have to eat their "nays." Hundreds of people chose to buy a home in Regent Park in that first launch, and thousands more have chosen to live in Regent Park over the following years.

VERSE SEVENTEEN

FISHING FOR COMMERCIAL PARTNERS

With the success of the One Cole launch under our belt and the benefit of a slowly improving economy, we were confident that "if we build it, they will come" would work for residential uses.

On the flip side, however, leasing commercial spaces would be another mountain to climb. Who would set up shop in a neighbourhood known for guns and gangs rather than croissants and cortados?

Construction was well underway at One Cole, along with a significant retail component wrapping the corner at Parliament and Dundas Streets. Empty storefronts would be a terrible signal. With that in mind, we charted an intentional course to fill three must-have retail uses at the base of One Cole: a grocery store, bank, and coffee shop.

The dramatic Sobeys story had a happy FreshCo ending, but we needed to secure the other must-haves adjacent to the 27,000-square-foot anchor grocery store.

Although there was a cheque-cashing outlet nearby, complete with prison-like bars on the windows, there hadn't been a bank branch in

Regent Park in over fifty years, and the nearest grocery store was blocks away. A cup of coffee? Forget about it.

Don Pugh and Nicole Ferrari of our commercial leasing team leaned into this mission with gusto.

Pugh has been a partner at Daniels for thirty-four years and has worn many hats over the decades, including leadership of our low-rise housing operation. Along with Simona Annibale, Pugh spearheaded our "First Home" division, creating the most affordable ownership opportunities in the GTA. Along the way, Pugh also established and ran our property management and residential leasing divisions.

THE BANK

We had relationships with all the big banks, and each one responded positively to this opportunity. RBC had always been number one, and Jennifer Tory, a senior executive at the bank, made the momentous decision to publicly plant RBC's flag in the neighbourhood.

RBC committed not only to a 3,600-square-foot branch but also to organizing a job fair immediately. Jennifer was ready to rock and roll on day one, and her team hired and trained local residents at existing RBC branches prior to opening the branch in Regent Park.

Fast-forward to a memorable moment when Jennifer brought then RBC CEO Gord Nixon to the opening celebration. Mr. Nixon, an icon of the Canadian business community, spent time chatting with branch manager Jasmina Zdravkovic and every member of the branch team, most of whom had walked to work that morning from around the corner.

This was deeply symbolic. The message to the community and the city at large was clear: RBC, Canada's largest bank, is here, the revitalization is real, so let's all get on board to make it a success.

Subsequently, following an energetic full community walkabout with CIBC CEO Victor Dodig and team, CIBC joined RBC as an active construction lending partner. Rounding out the roster of big banks engaged in the revitalization, Scotiabank has now opened a branch, and BMO will be opening a branch in the community in 2025.

THE COFFEE SHOP

One of many takeaways from our early "listen and learn" tour was the importance of bringing a coffee shop to Regent Park. Every neighbourhood in the city has multiple coffee shops. Regent Park had none.

David Adcock, executive director of Yonge Street Mission (YSM), was a strong advocate for building community wealth. His vision was to create a locally owned coffee shop that would become a significant platform for local economic development. We agreed wholeheartedly.

As a result, David and I, together with Dixon Hall's Kate Stark, marched across the city looking for an angel investor to underwrite the purchase of a coffee franchise. We needed $300,000 to make it work. Unfortunately, we came up empty-handed.

Without cash in hand, we pitched co-ownership and other variations to Second Cup and Timothy's... to no avail. Tim Hortons, however, didn't shut the door immediately, which led to a meeting with the bigwigs at their head office. Another big boardroom table, and another no to community ownership.

However, the head office team introduced us to Farhan Basharat, an existing franchise operator at Parliament and Wellesley Streets and their chosen franchisee for Regent Park. Together, we hammered out a long-term employment and training collaboration with YSM.

It was a wonderful moment when the first Timmies opened at the corner of Parliament and Cole, with fourteen of fifteen team members being from the community. Basharat has been a supportive commercial partner and local employer ever since and has welcomed many young people from the community to Tims Camps programs over the years, in addition to making an annual charitable donation to YSM for the first term of the lease.

THE TELECOMMUNICATIONS PARTNER

Finding a telecommunications partner proved easier than anticipated. We started with an informal bid process to the major providers. Although Bell and Telus submitted decent proposals, Michael Krstajic, vice president of national field sales at Rogers Communications, was prepared to go the distance and brought chairman Edward Rogers to our office to demonstrate intent.

Michael and Edward, accompanied by Rich Young, Daniels' account manager, made it clear that Regent Park was in their backyard and that Rogers was going to be with us for the long term as a true "city-building" partner.

In short, Rogers Communications put together a compelling package for both our condominium purchasers and TCH tenants, including a commitment to a storefront retail operation. As a sweetener, Rogers agreed to also provide state-of-the art broadcast equipment to Regent Park FOCUS to help establish RPTV, a locally produced television station, along with a cash contribution that enabled FOCUS to create a home within a city-owned hub at 40 Regent Street, subsequently expanding into Daniels Spectrum.

Although Adonis Huggins wasn't able to realize the dream of a dedicated cable channel throughout the community, the evolution of YouTube allowed FOCUS to grow RPTV as a powerful platform for local storytelling. Today, new generations of young people from the community produce three hours of original content weekly for RPTV, with over forty thousand views annually.

The Dreamers Peace Garden, 2012.

VERSE EIGHTEEN

TRAUMA, SADNESS, ANGER, HOPE

S O MUCH WAS GOING WELL, despite the challenges. We were leasing spaces, tenants were beginning to see positive outcomes, condo owners were calling the community "home," and new amenities were in place, with more on the way.

And then on June 2, 2012, a young man fired fourteen bullets into the crowded food court at the Eaton Centre. Six people were hurt and two young men were killed, one of whom—Nixon Nirmalendran—grew up in Regent Park.

It was devastating for family members and residents. The entire community felt the trauma and a deep well of sadness. Retaliation was a real possibility, and people feared that a wave of violence would spread. Inevitably, some were also angry that the disruption and dislocation caused by the revitalization was part of the problem. Social systems that had existed for decades, whether healthy or not, had been ripped apart.

Resilience is often cited as a goal in building strong communities—bouncing back and moving forward. We experienced that resilience first-hand in the aftermath of the Eaton Centre shooting.

The inaugural Show Love event, hosted by Kenneth Slater of Dixon Hall and Seema Jethalal of Toronto Artscape Inc. (Artscape), inspired me to write our friends in the community and all the partners engaged in this challenging work.

June 16, 2012
Hello everyone,

The last few weeks have been very tough for all residents of Regent Park, and for everyone working so hard to support, nurture, and help make the revitalization a success. It was never going to be easy. There was never a simple, clear path, with all the steps numbered for all of us to follow.

This has never been as clear as it is this morning. Although the revitalization is working on so many levels, the tragic Eaton Centre shooting and resultant "guns and gangs" narrative in the media is going to make all of our work that much more difficult.

There are, however, so many reasons for hope, for optimism, and for not only staying the course but also renewing our efforts with full force and determination.

Yesterday afternoon, for example, I had yet another opportunity to experience the strength and resilience of the Regent Park community. As friends and relatives returned to "the Park" from Nixon Nirmalendran's funeral, they found their neighbours reclaiming a long neglected open space within the community. Kenneth Slater of Dixon Hall and Seema Jethalal of Artscape put out the word and residents responded, coming together to make a strong statement.

Side by side, pulling weeds and planting flowers, people of all ages were showing love for each other and their community. One young person, perhaps nine years old, worked very hard to pull out a particularly difficult, deeply rooted weed. With much effort, pulling hard and excavating deeply around it with a bread knife, she succeeded.

It was a very inspiring moment, clearly demonstrating how grief and adversity can be channelled into positive action.

There are so many positive stories to tell, and all of us need to tell them. We can't sit back and simply let others voice their often ill-informed opinions.

Most importantly, the world needs to know that the vision and underlying foundation are strong, that the revitalization is based on principles that came from the community, from the "ground" in Regent Park, and that everyone involved is committed to seeing that vision through to a successful completion.

I trust that all of you will continue spreading the word, reaching out to media, to your colleagues and board members, to "influencers" in the broader community, to friends and relatives, such that many strong, informed voices will be heard.

Be well.
MC

BRIDGE
Show Love

People coming together to simply show love became a powerful force within the neighbourhood... food, music, drumming circles, conversation. Reflection. Mourning. Sorrow. Friendship.

Henry Heillig and I wrote "Show Love" not long after that first gathering. We took it into the Canterbury Studio with Kenneth Slater and Nation Cheong playing percussion.

We also found other ways to support and bring others to the table. Tolias, our landscape maintenance contractor, donated flowers, soil, and mulch. Our painters donated paint, and we provided funding for a weekly Show Love gathering through the course of that summer and a few summers since.

For some time, Dixon Hall operated the Show Love café within Daniels Spectrum, and "show love" remains an important message that resonates throughout the community.

"SHOW LOVE" from *The Journey Musical*

Young men, young men, so many young men gone.
    In sisters, in brothers, in mothers, memories live on...

There's headlines, storylines, reporters on the doorstep.
    Cameras and questions, politicians in lockstep.
This doesn't help, it's not what we need... how long will this go on?

How do you show love in a time of grieving? How do you show love in a time of loss?

By planting trees, planting flowers, pulling weeds, you and Hope,
    side by side, spending hopeful hours.
By playing drums, fixing the playground, just by being around.

How do you show love in a time of grieving? How do you show love in a time of loss?

We bring the food, you light the barbeque,
In the park, day and night, light and dark, life goes on.

Sometimes it's just being there, without words, just being around.

VERSE NINETEEN

PHASE TWO AND BEYOND

T**he certainty of** an "all phases" contract extension allowed us to think long term, to be creative with all the intersecting building blocks. Without that certainty, we would have been building a few buildings rather than a community.

Although Tim Hortons was under construction in Phase One, we wanted to land an independent coffee operation in Phase Two. Unfortunately, none of the cool-cat operators were willing to leap into the deep at such an early stage. Yes, there was construction activity at the corner of Dundas and Parliament Streets, but the balance of the revitalization was nothing more than artist renderings and our trusty scale model of the community. Dundas Street was years away from becoming more than a place to drive through without stopping.

With several "thanks but no thanks" answers from independent coffee operators, we decided to go big or go home.

From that crazy thought emerged the vision of a bistro that would become a place to hang out during the day and double as a training facility and hub for local caterers. In the evening, the bistro would turn into a destination for great music, a compelling reason for people to linger a little longer in Regent Park.

Tom Dutton brought our colleague Brock Stevenson into the forefront of our design team, and together with Don Schmitt and the team from Diamond Schmitt Architects, we began designing a mixed-use development at the corner of Dundas and Sackville Streets. The overall plan included a twenty-six-storey condominium rising above a hypothetical food service operation with outdoor patios on both frontages, along with a super-cool ice cream window fronting onto Dundas. The restaurant included two kitchens, one "front of house" to support the bistro, and one, much larger, "back of house," envisioned as a home for a catering business and/or food-related entrepreneurship hub.

We also took a leap of faith by envisioning office space above the bistro. Market intelligence was telling us that leasing office space in Regent Park was as likely as establishing an affordable housing colony on Mars. Despite that feedback, we needed to walk the talk on creating a complete community, with office space playing a pivotal role, providing connective tissue between retail and residential, between daytime and nighttime uses.

This is the essence of what Tom Dutton and I have done over the past thirty-plus years: take hypotheticals and turn them into living, breathing, functioning places within our city.

SOLO

TOM DUTTON

Tom and I have made beautiful music together for thirty-six years, both literally and figuratively.

We met at a national co-op housing conference in Alberta in the early '80s. Tom was developing affordable housing in Halifax, and I was with CHFT in Toronto. After spending the day discussing the future of the co-op movement, it was time to party. Unfortunately, the bluegrass band hired to entertain that evening was far from entertaining.

When the band took a break, Tom asked one of the guitar players if he could strum a little. I was on the other side of the room and—*kaboom!* There were some incredibly soulful sounds coming from the stage, and it wasn't the band. It was Tom Dutton singing and playing the blues. By brilliant happenstance, there was an old upright piano on the far side of the banquet hall.

And it was a message from the heavens that the piano was not only playable but also in tune. I started playing along, and the party picked up tremendous momentum. Tom and I have been jamming ever since.

When I left CHFT and began building a team at Daniels, Tom was my first call. After moving his family to Mississauga in 1987, Tom led both our design and construction teams, conceiving and building close to forty thousand homes and condominiums, including TIFF Bell Lightbox, one of the most significant cultural institutions in Canada.

The much-beloved Paintbox Bistro at Dundas and Sackville.

VERSE TWENTY

PAINTBOX BISTRO: MORE THAN A COFFEE SHOP

IT TOOK A LOT OF WORK to turn all those hypotheticals into a cup of coffee. We approached many of Toronto's prominent restaurateurs, all of whom kicked the tires and then wished us well. The stigma associated with the neighbourhood was a tough nut to crack.

I even took the bold step of reaching out to Jamie Oliver, who had just established Fifteen in Europe, a training ground for young people from challenged neighbourhoods hoping to build a career in the food services industry. His people called back and also wished us well.

And then, as we were pushing this concept up an enormous mountain, heaven sent us Brenda Pipitone and Luigi Ferrara of George Brown College. Anne Sado, then the college's president, encouraged Brenda and Luigi to build a strong bridge between her community college and our work in the community. Brenda, as director of community partnerships, and Luigi, as dean of the college's Centre for Arts, Design and Information Technology, were both intent on partnering on a host of initiatives under the umbrella of the revitalization. The two mobilized dean John Walker

SOLO

LORRAINE SEGATO

It was a powerful message to have Lorraine Segato, one of Canada's greatest artists, living in the community for two years as Regent Park's inaugural artist-in-residence. Her local programming at Daniels Spectrum and Paintbox Bistro was outstanding, as were the many mentorships she undertook during her tenure, including the powerful "Rise Up" remix featuring Regent Park's breakout artist Mustafa.

Although she is recognized globally for co-writing and performing "Rise Up" and other classics with the Parachute Club, Lorraine's quiet work in supporting non-profit initiatives across the country has inspired me and so many others.

Lorraine was named to the Order of Canada in 2022, and her band, the Parachute Club, was inducted into Canada's Walk of Fame in 2023.

and chef John Higgins of George Brown's Centre for Hospitality and Culinary Arts, leading us to chef Chris Klugman, an instructor at the school.

And thus began the story of Klugman's Paintbox Bistro, an independent café that became a beloved social enterprise and community gathering place. Paintbox was a place to meet and hang but also to learn, with Chef Chris welcoming over a hundred women to his catering kitchen to achieve their food handling certification.

Tom Dutton and I also worked hard to entice Toronto's foremost music impresarios to create a new room for great music. We toured multiple music industry guests in hard hats and steel-toe boots through the concrete shell of what would become Paintbox Bistro.

Alas, none of those seeds took root, so we did what we do when hitting a brick wall—we climbed over it. Yes, we did it ourselves, with Henry Heillig, and subsequently Greg Gooding, curating a series of outstanding jazz shows. We also partnered with Ray and Rochelle Koskie's Jazz Performance and Education Centre, energizing the room over a series of shows. A who's who list of Canadian jazz musicians played at Paintbox, including Archie Alleyne, Jackie Richardson, Phil Dwyer, Jane Bunnett, Joe Sealy, and, of course, Henry Heillig's quartet, Heillig Manoeuvre.

The jazz series was followed by hip hop shows curated by Miles Jones, interspersed with the memorable cabaret series Wild Women (Don't Get the Blues), hosted by Lorraine Segato, Regent Park's first artist-in-residence. Segato brought chef Greg Couillard to entice audiences with his food creations, as well as a powerful lineup of friends and award-winning performers from the industry.

Shakura S'Aida, iskwē, Alana Bridgewater, Michelle Willis, Diane Flacks, Roula Said, Suzie Vinnick, Lyne Tremblay, Miku Graham,

Shawnee Talbot, Diane Leah, and Saidah Baba Talibah, now known as SATE, graced the stage at the Bistro. Stacie McGregor was resident keyboard player for the series, and Colleen Allen on horns gave Segato and her Wild Women artists a solid foundation on which to groove.

Notably, Segato also welcomed a local Regent Park artist into each Wild Women show, including spoken-word artists Trevlyn Kennedy and Britta B., as well as Regent Park School of Music graduate Charlotte Siegel, a young soprano now performing on the big stage at the Canadian Opera Company.

And with a little help from JazzFM, families and kids also flocked to the Junior Jazz Jam Series for kids at the Bistro.

The bottom line: it all worked. From jazz to hip hop to the Wild Women series, great artists brought audiences, and those audiences spread the word. All of this spoke volumes. Regent Park wasn't scary at all. In fact, it was a place to experience exceptional music for people of all ages and backgrounds, performed by the best artists in the country.

Chef Klugman and Paintbox Bistro were important fixtures in the evolution of the revitalization. Unfortunately, COVID was a tough pill for all restaurants to swallow, and after ten years of serving great food and coffee, and hosting myriad local events, we all said a fond farewell to Chef Chris and the Paintbox team.

Before leaving, however, Chef Chris did us a solid by introducing us to the Gusto 54 Restaurant Group. Janet Zuccarini, Juanita Dickson, Tyler Rutherford, Lindsay Stevenson, Georgia Zimbel, and the rest of team Gusto recognized the potential of the "new" Regent Park and opened Café ZUZU in the fall of 2022.

BRIDGE

"Don't Go Out Tonight"

The first performance at Paintbox Bistro was a celebration of Archie Alleyne's eightieth birthday on January 11, 2013. It was a particularly poignant moment in the life of the revitalization.

Archie was one of the greatest jazz drummers of all time, having played with Billie Holiday, Stan Getz, Lester Young, and a long list of other top-tier artists. At the time, Archie was living upstairs in the Paintbox condominiums and had adopted the Bistro as his home away from home.

Archie and Jackie Richardson had just finished their sound check in preparation for our first-ever show. They sounded amazing. The room sounded amazing. We had done it—built a room for outstanding music in Regent Park. Chef Chris served delicious Paintbox coffee, and we sat in the front window contemplating the next big question: Would anyone come?

As we sipped and chatted, the sound of police and ambulance sirens rattled our reveries. A few minutes later, we learned that a young man had been shot and killed in the stairwell of a TCH building just down the street from where we were sitting.

As we were stepping into the future, we were struck by a stark reminder that young people in the neighbourhood were still at risk, perhaps even more so because of the displacement, the disruption that the revitalization was causing.

A few days later, I met Barry Thomas, the heart and soul of TCH's community development team, for a coffee at Paintbox. Barry's roots in the neighbourhood were deep. He knew everyone, including the young man who had died from gunshot wounds a few days earlier.

With a heavy heart and deep sadness in his eyes, Barry told me that it had been two hundred days since the last young man from the neighbourhood had been killed.

That moment hit me like a ton of bricks. Although seven years into the revitalization process, the painful fact that Barry counted days between these tragedies was a powerful reminder that the work of the revitalization had only just begun.

"DON'T GO OUT TONIGHT" from *The Journey Musical*

It's been 200 days, 200 days since you walked out the door.
200 days, 200 days, I don't wanna count no more.
You know there's trouble out there, you know there's trouble out there.

I know what I know, little brother... don't go out tonight.
You got nothing to prove, you've got everything to lose.
Even if you win you lose, little brother... don't go out tonight.

Don't go out in the night, little brother, don't go out tonight.
Don't go out in the night, little brother, into the arms of a fight.

I begged, I pleaded, said "Little bro you're needed," I did what a sister could.
You looked at me, so silently, a tough kid from the neighbourhood.

I stared you down, you stepped around, I cried, "Don't go out tonight."
I grabbed your arm, you pushed me down, and disappeared into the night.

You went out that night, little brother, now every night is a haze.
You didn't come home, little brother, left me counting days.

Could I have saved him? Would that I could. Never could forget him, and never would.
Get back to the living, not counting days. Get back to the living, not counting days...

VERSE TWENTY-ONE

MORE BIG CHALLENGES: INTERNAL FORCES

A GLOBAL ECONOMIC MELTDOWN was tough to predict. So were the political interventions that have impacted continuity and momentum along the path.

Just as residents were settling into their new homes and getting to know each other, our partner in the revitalization was gone. There was no CEO, no board of directors—no one was home at Toronto Community Housing.

What happened? Simple answer: Rob Ford was elected mayor of Toronto.

Throughout his campaign for the 2010 election, Ford depicted TCH as a "gravy train" that needed to be stopped in its tracks. Once he was in the mayor's chair, that narrative provided cover to fire TCH's acting CEO Keiko Nakamura as well as the entire board of directors. The new mayor also fired Derek Ballantyne from his appointment as COO of Build Toronto, an agency established to create value within the City's real estate portfolio.

This was a major turning point for the team left standing at TCH. Everyone was frozen in time and space, unwilling to make a decision that could result in an "off with their head" edict from the mayor's office.

On our side of the day-to-day work of the revitalization, the spirit of collaboration and partnership was blown to smithereens.

In an effort to further eviscerate the housing company, Mayor Ford invited *Toronto Sun* reporter Sue-Ann Levy on his weekly Sunday radio show, providing oxygen to several front-page articles in which Ms. Levy attacked and undermined the foundation of the Daniels/TCH partnership. In short, Ms. Levy accused Councillor Pam McConnell, Derek Ballantyne, and many of us at Daniels of gaming the system, of buying the best suites at One Cole at below-market prices before offering them to the public.

Initially, we huddled with our partners at TCH to address these totally unfounded accusations. One minute we were planning a press conference where we would stand shoulder to shoulder to counter Ms. Levy's outrageous claims. And the next we were toast, without the courtesy of a call to explain why we were being thrown under the bus. Political roadkill.

Instead, at a TCH-only media event, board chair Bud Purves announced the appointment of retired Ontario chief justice Patrick LeSage to lead an inquiry that would probe every aspect of our partnership and the overall Regent Park revitalization.

The impact, on both a personal and corporate level, hurt badly, with both local and national media picking up the story. The *National Post*, for example, had this to say on March 28, 2012: "In a series of articles published this week by *Toronto Sun* columnist Sue-Ann Levy,

TCHC executives, as well as Toronto city councillor Pam McConnell and project developer Mitch Cohen, are accused of buying up choice condos in One Cole."[2]

The community was outraged. Approximately 150 residents hosted their own press conference a few days after the Purves announcement. Debra Dineen and Diane MacLean spoke passionately about their community and the progress that had been made. MacLean, for example, stated clearly: "Together, we're changing this neighbourhood for the better. We're building a new Regent Park." Kate Sellar, a new homeowner at One Cole, had this to say: "Someday soon, people are going to stop asking if this community, as an experiment, works. It's not an experiment. It's our home."[3]

Although the arguments were passionate and heartfelt, it was too late. The City and housing company had set sail with their judicial inquiry. And thus began five months of brutal interrogations. The clear assumption throughout, projected by LeSage's five-person legal team, was that we were guilty.

Finally, after living this non-stop nightmare, I received a call late one night from Gene Jones, the fourth CEO on TCH's ever-evolving leadership roster. Mr. Jones had just read the LeSage report and was calling with a heads-up. Jones prefaced his remarks by saying, "There's going to be a lot of very angry people at city hall when the news breaks in the morning."

As we knew it would, the report found zero wrongdoing. The whole thing had been an enormous nothing sandwich, albeit at a cost to the public purse of $125,000 in legal fees, as well as the impact on our personal and corporate reputations. It was also a significant distraction for TCH, which was, in itself, a terrible disservice to tenants across the city.

Predictably, the *Toronto Sun* buried the report, in which Justice LeSage was highly complimentary of the public/private partnership between Daniels and TCH:

> Daniels was prepared to take a risk and has done more than required, in the sense of building a community and getting involved in charitable programs. They have provided a conduit to the commercial partners participating in the Revitalization Project. In my view, TCHC and Daniels may be proud of their accomplishment.[4]

VERSE TWENTY-TWO

FIGHTING TO STAY THE COURSE

THE CEO'S CHAIR AT TCH must be a very uncomfortable place, and understandably so. Managing 58,000 social housing units with a $3 billion repair backlog would be a daunting assignment for anyone. Since 2006, that chair has welcomed and subsequently said goodbye to CEOs at an alarming rate. Here today, gone the next. A total of fourteen CEOs thus far.

Coincidentally, or not, Gene Jones was ousted from the top job shortly after I received his call. Jones, a strong leader with deep experience managing municipal housing companies in the US, was brought in to refresh corporate leadership and reboot the efficacy of the corporation. After kick-starting that process, Jones was unceremoniously given the boot.

Greg Spearn, the corporation's chief development officer, was asked to step in as acting CEO. Spearn was one of the most effective leaders we encountered. However, as acting CEO, he was allowed to rest only one cheek on the big chair and was seriously constrained in his ability to build a senior executive team. Despite the constraints, and late-night calls from Mayor Ford intervening on behalf of an individual tenant, Spearn's team performed herculean work across the portfolio, bringing tangible results to residents.

With decades of private-sector real estate experience, Spearn understood the importance of continuity and momentum. He also understood the power of the public/private partnership model and was willing to entertain a refresh of the agreement that had been so successful in Phases One and Two.

In April 2017, shortly after John Tory succeeded Rob Ford, Martin Blake and I tabled a formal proposal to renew our "all phases" contract with Spearn and Chris Eby, Mayor Tory's chief of staff. We proposed to renew the "all phases" contract that had been terminated on Mayor Ford's watch. In addition to the terms of a renewed partnership agreement, our proposal incorporated a "case for continuity," outlining why the "all phases" contract established in April 2009 should be reinstated.

> **CONCLUDING STATEMENT OF THE "CASE FOR CONTINUITY"**
>
> April 2017
>
> There is a very strong case for TCH to work through to the end of the revitalization with Daniels. TCH's long-term partnership with Daniels has not only generated international accolades, but also enormous value to TCH and the City of Toronto as a whole, well beyond what could have been achieved with a tendering process for successive phases.
>
> Great cities are built on the foundation of a long-term vision, not a stop and start mentality using only dollars as the singular measure to evaluate success. In Regent Park today, success can be measured in myriad ways.
>
> There is no doubt that both the short- and long-term financial returns to TCH have greatly exceeded expectations. As important,

however, is the creation of enormous community capital, which is absolutely critical to ensure long-term value within the neighbourhood, and in the relationship of this neighbourhood to the entire city.

Twelve years ago, people from the broader city were afraid to set foot in Regent Park. Today, they enjoy a meal and jazz at Paintbox Bistro, theatrical productions at Daniels Spectrum, swimming at the Aquatic Centre, and running on the new track at the Athletic Grounds.

Today, people from beyond the neighbourhood come to Regent Park to see a doctor at the Sumac Creek Family Health Centre, to give birth at the Toronto Birthing Centre, or to watch a movie Under the Stars in the big park under the auspices of the Regent Park Film Festival.

Today, residents of Regent Park are proud of their community, proud to show off their new homes, and proud to see friends and relatives working at FreshCo by Sobeys or at the local RBC branch.

A neighbourhood transformation of this nature is not a short game, but rather must be nurtured slowly, deliberately, and with great intentionality. It doesn't happen by happenstance, or by accident, but rather through the implementation of a shared vision over the long term.

Many years ago, an arts and cultural centre wasn't even on the radar. Nor was the Athletic Grounds, which includes a soccer pitch, a basketball court, an outdoor running track, and a refurbished hockey rink. They exist today, as true jewels in the revitalization crown, because TCH harnessed the creativity and socially progressive entrepreneurial spirit of their private sector partner.

Today, we must focus that creativity and spirit on Phases 4/5, on the creation of additional value for the residents of Regent Park, TCH, and the City of Toronto as a whole.

> Today, we are poised to weave the final strands together in the tapestry of the Regent Park revitalization and look forward to doing so through an extension of our partnership with Toronto Community Housing.

Shortly after presenting our proposal to Mayor Tory's team, acting CEO Spearn was handed the pink slip, bringing conversations about renewing our contract to a screeching halt.

The oddity—or perhaps absurdity—was that Spearn had applied for the permanent position with written support from every operating unit manager plus the three primary unions operating within TCH. Notwithstanding that support, he was turfed and literally escorted out of the building, despite three productive years piloting the ship.

The hiring process for the next CEO took forever, which was no surprise. It was a daunting challenge, and several candidates took a pass. Board chair Kevin Marshman stepped in as acting CEO until the job search team landed on Kathy Milsom, who took the big chair in early September 2017.

We wrote Ms. Milsom on her first day, asking for a meeting to discuss the future of the revitalization. For reasons unfathomable, Ms. Milsom was unable to meet us until more than three months later. That was remarkable: Regent Park was the most significant revitalization in TCH's portfolio, and the new CEO was too busy to meet us.

We finally met on December 18, 2017, at Paintbox Bistro. In the background, Chef Klugman was running a food handling certification program for members of the Regent Park Catering Collective.

Martin Blake and I were pumped, ready to outline all the reasons TCH should re-embrace the partnership model that had achieved such remarkable success. Continuity. Momentum. Collaboration. Partnership. Success. Delivery. On time and on budget. Trust within the neighbourhood. There were myriad powerful reasons to stay the course.

After a few brief moments of chit-chat, we got down to the business at hand. Martin launched into the fifty ways we had done right by our partner and the community, through thick and thin, in sickness and health. Ms. Milsom raised her hand before Martin reached second base and launched into her own highly scripted narrative: TCH loved us dearly. We were exceptional partners doing brilliant work.

With that preamble, we knew another shoe was about to drop, and drop it did: the marriage was over. The partnership would not be renewed. The meeting ended abruptly, after nine minutes and thirty-six seconds. Ms. Milsom left her tea steaming on the table, dwarfed by the steam rising to the rafters from our side of the table.

The new CEO did, however, leave us with an upside: if we wanted, we were welcome to participate in a proposal call for the final two phases.

That was a real slap in the face. After years of creating value, bringing a world of commitment to the table, we were being told "See ya never, it's been swell."

VERSE TWENTY-THREE

ON THE LOSING END

After some deep soul-searching, we did respond to the proposal call for Phases Four and Five. Unfortunately, we came out on the losing end, despite putting our best foot forward. On the surface, we were outbid by a country mile, which resulted in walking around for months thereafter muttering Bob Dylan's famous words "Money doesn't talk, it swears."

We felt very good about that "best foot" we put forward. Our proposal built on everything we had learned, outlining a long list of investments we would make immediately and in each successive year until completion. These front-end investments were in direct response to real-time needs, seeding local programs and enterprises in the present.

In addition to responding to a host of real-time needs with cash investments, our proposal incorporated a training centre in partnership with Carpenters Local 27 and the College of Carpenters and Allied Trades. Our long-term partnership with Mike Yorke and the carpenters' union has resulted in long-standing careers within the construction industry for many Regent Park residents.

A significant challenge, and cost, was getting young people from Regent Park up to Local 27's existing training facility north of the city. Establishing a training facility focussed on mass timber and sustainability in the heart of the city would have been a game changer for an industry in desperate need of a makeover.

We expressed our deep disappointment as well as our ongoing commitment to the Regent Park community in an open letter to local residents and the city at large.

> **AN OPEN LETTER**
>
> Toronto, December 15, 2020
>
> The Daniels Corporation has been Toronto Community Housing's (TCH) development partner on the Regent Park revitalization over the past fifteen years. Recently, we learned that TCH has chosen another developer for the final two phases of the revitalization.
>
> Although we are deeply disappointed, we wish TCH and their new partner well. We also want to reassure local residents of our long-term commitment to the Regent Park community. Our work has never been just about sewers, roads, buildings, or district energy systems. It has been about building community.
>
> As we complete our work in Phase Three, we will continue to invest substantial resources, further solidifying the foundation we've built together with the local community. Empowerment, engagement, social procurement, and building community capital have been highly intentional building blocks every step of the way, and through that process the threads of social cohesion are beginning to take root.

The revitalization didn't start at City Hall or at Toronto Community Housing. It started in Regent Park, with local voices at the heart of the conversation. Today, more than ever, it is essential that those voices are heard and respected.

Looking back, we recall the day in February 2006 when the first buildings were demolished, kicking off a truly historic journey. At that time, most residents felt considerable anxiety as their homes and histories were obliterated for the promise of a better tomorrow. As the wrecking ball knocked down those first buildings, very few people predicted success.

Today, the revitalization is celebrated as the gold standard by which a challenged inner-city neighbourhood can be transformed. In fact, the Government of Canada and UN Habitat recently announced the Regent Park World Urban Pavilion, situated intentionally in Regent Park, as a model of inclusive urbanism for cities around the world to emulate.

Over the past fifteen years, Regent Park has been reconnected to the city and a thriving mixed-use, mixed-income, multi-generational community is gaining strength and momentum. Significant new amenities are in place, including a six-acre park, Aquatic Centre, Community Centre, the Regent Park Athletic Grounds, and Daniels Spectrum, a 60,000-square-foot arts and cultural hub.

The revitalization has also been a catalyst for inclusive local economic opportunity, with Toronto Employment and Social Services (TESS) reporting that 580 jobs have been created as a direct result of the revitalization. We want to thank our sub-contractors, service providers, and consultants for opening their doors and their hearts to residents of Regent Park.

We also want to express our appreciation to the financial institutions, commercial tenants, post-secondary institutions, non-profit agencies, charitable foundations, and individual philanthropists for embracing the partnership model that has set the stage for long-term success.

Looking ahead, we hope that many more partners will come to the table, lending expertise as well as financial resources in order to see the revitalization through to successful completion.

All of us at Daniels are proud of what we've accomplished, and of our partnership with this remarkable community. We're incredibly fortunate to have made so many lifelong friends along the way.

The Regent Park revitalization is an opportunity for Toronto to truly get it right, to shine a light around the world, illuminating what can be achieved when collaboration and partnership take centre stage, and when development is about achieving positive outcomes for all stakeholders.

Mitchell Cohen, President & CEO
The Daniels Corporation

SET FOUR

A CRESCENDO OF SOCIAL INFRASTRUCTURE

VERSE TWENTY-FOUR

EMERGING COMMUNITY LEADERS

F ROM AN ISOLATED "garden city" to becoming part of the city, the transformation unfolded with twists and turns generated by politics, the economy, and the inherent challenges of partnering with a public-sector agency that is wholly owned by the municipality.

We knew we could design, build, and sell market condominiums. We also knew we could deliver outstanding replacement rental buildings to TCH. Our design, estimating, contracting, and construction teams were the strongest in the industry. Tom Dutton, Sam Tassone, Gokul Pisharoty, Antonella Spano, and Brock Stevenson were on the inside, with my son, Jake Cohen, now chief operating officer, leading our implementation team. And with Steve Langdon, Brian Merkley, Andrew Marson, and Ian Nastor leading our field teams, we were well positioned to deliver the goods.

The social infrastructure side, on the other hand, was a new mountain to climb. Building social cohesion is a challenge in any community. Doing so within a community in the throes of being torn apart and put together again is a challenge on steroids.

SOLO

DEANY PETERS

Deany Peters has been an active participant in the life of Regent Park since the day she moved in with her three children in the early 1980s. Deany was one of the first participants in the Regent Park Community Worker Training Project, a groundbreaking initiative addressing the sad fact that local service agencies generally didn't hire from within communities in which they delivered service. One of Deany's placements was at the Regent Park Community Health Centre, which ultimately led to a lengthy career, including as the centre's first community development worker. In addition to her work at the centre, Deany has been an active volunteer, activist, and respected local leader for decades. Deany welcomed me into her world with warmth and enthusiasm on my first foray into Regent Park, and it warms my heart to watch and experience the love and energy she invests in her community.

Over the years, it has been inspiring to witness the evolution of many local leaders, each bringing enormous personal energy to the work of building community. These residents, some new to the community and some who have lived in Regent Park for decades, have worked tirelessly, building an engagement and governance framework that continues to evolve as the revitalization unfolds. The work is hard and tiring, and everyone is learning on the job, except in this case the job is being done by volunteers, out of a desire to build a strong community.

Many local leaders have participated in endless meetings, formal and informal, often challenging the City, TCH, and Daniels to step up, do more, and listen more thoughtfully. All of them, including Deany Peters, Ines Garcia, Marlene DeGenova, Gail Lynch, and the Afrah twins, Ibrahim and Ismail, have helped fill our knowledge gaps, guiding us along the path.

SOLO

INES GARCIA

Ines was one of the first residents I met after entering our partnership agreement with TCH. Like many in the community, Ines was somewhat skeptical that anything good would come from the endless meetings and committee work. And she let me know that very clearly on several occasions in those early years.

Despite her hesitation, Ines was always there, at every meeting and social gathering, asking questions, chasing answers, and holding our feet to the fire in order to ensure the best outcomes for local residents.

At Sunday in the Park, Taste of Regent Park, community bazaars, and at every gathering, Ines's spirit of community is always shining brightly, often with her candy floss and popcorn machines flossing and popping. And of course, there are her large serving platters filled with her famously delicious empanadas.

Opinionated, strong-willed, and passionate about family and community, Ines has become a dear friend over the course of the revitalization.

SOLO

MARLENE DEGENOVA

Marlene DeGenova was an early adopter, excited by the opportunity to become involved in the evolution of the community. A former costume designer who built her own business-to-business marketing company, Marlene did significant due diligence prior to purchasing a suite in Paintbox Condominiums.

Part of that diligence was to look carefully at the scale model depicting how the Paintbox building related to other buildings in direct proximity. With careful consideration, Marlene chose a suite with unobstructed views to the south.

All was well until my Wite-Out wiped out a TCH building to make room for a potential arts and cultural centre (see Verse Thirty). We had to replace that density somewhere, and part of the reallocation wiped out Marlene's unobstructed view.

Thus began a series of emotional conversations between Martin Blake and Marlene, a purchaser who had made an investment in good faith based on what we had shown her in our presentation centre. Yes, we had the legal right to move density around, but Marlene made it clear that we didn't have the moral right.

TCH was adamant that we couldn't lose density. Doing so could scupper the proposed cultural centre. We had to put the density somewhere, which led to a series of sculpting and resculpting exercises with Diamond Schmitt Architects, followed by meetings between Martin and Marlene. After considerable back-and-forth, we landed at a place where no one was happy, a true Canadian compromise, and Marlene has been living at Paintbox Condominiums ever since.

From those early encounters, Marlene grew into a prominent community leader, a condominium owner ready and willing to dive into the complex interpersonal web of community building. Over the years, Marlene has also become a good friend.

As co-chair of the Regent Park Neighbourhood Association, Marlene is deeply engaged in and committed to her community.

DUET

IBRAHIM AND ISMAIL AFRAH

The awesome Afrah twins grew up in Regent Park within the arc of the revitalization. Their family moved into the community in 2001, having arrived in Canada from Somalia after spending some time in Kenya. The boys were teenagers at the time, listening, learning, absorbing, and deeply engaged at every stage of the process.

Ibrahim brings an entrepreneurial spirit to everything he touches and has created several small businesses, including Coat Check 4 Change, as well as a residential and commercial cleaning service. As co-chair of the Community Building Communications Working Group, Ibrahim developed the Hello Neighbour app, enabling community agencies and residents to share information about events, job opportunities, local businesses, and more. Ibrahim also worked full-time in the neighbourhood as the event and volunteer coordinator at Fred Victor, which included responsibility for coordinating Taste of Regent Park over the summer months.

Ibrahim continues to be actively engaged in the revitalization process, acting as co-chair of the Regent Park Social Development Plan's Employment and Economic Development Table, as well as a community representative on the World Urban Pavilion Steering Committee. He is also the founder of Regent Park Social, which offers tours of the neighbourhood to groups from across the city and around the world interested in learning about the revitalization.

Ibrahim's twin brother, Ismail, has also been highly engaged in the community development process. A deep thinker and philosopher at heart, Ismail is always reading, studying, and looking at all aspects of any situation, empathetic to diverse points of view.

Ismail began his community engagement and development work in neighbourhood outreach with the Toronto Centre of Learning & Development and later became a social development coordinator with the Toronto Christian Resource Centre.

He has been a significant voice at the table as community governance practices have evolved, including acting as co-chair of the Regent Park Neighbourhood Association alongside Marlene DeGenova. Like his brother, he has also co-chaired the Employment and Economic Development Table and participates on the World Urban Pavilion Committee.

Recently, Ismail took on full-time work for TCH in Alexandra Park as a community revitalization assistant. As a TCH employee, Ismail has had to recuse himself from many of the discussions around community benefits flowing from Phases Four and Five, as well as other issues that would present a conflict.

Both Ismail and Ibrahim were relocated to St. James Town when their Regent Park homes came up for demolition, but both have since exercised their "right of return" and are back in the community with their families.

Passion for community. Commitment. Inquisitive. Energetic community builders. These are the Brothers Afrah, and it is a blessing to have their positive energy flowing through the community.

SOLO

GAIL LYNCH

Gail's name was mentioned to me many times before I met her. I had heard that she had moved into one of our condominium buildings and had immediately become deeply involved in the life and evolution of the community. We met for the first time at Daniels Spectrum. I was working at my computer in the community living room. Gail was working at hers. We struck up a conversation that day and have been having deep conversations ever since about the meaning of community and how to build a place in which everyone is heard and everyone belongs. I also learned about her incredible entrepreneurial spirit and the evolution of Zero Cocktail Bar, a brilliant non-alcoholic pop-up creation that pops up at social gatherings throughout Regent Park and beyond. Each of Gail's non-alcoholic cocktails is a work of art. In fact, Gail is a work of art, bringing style, love, warmth, and positivity to every conversation and interaction.

VERSE TWENTY-FIVE

PRIMARY ORGANIZING ELEMENTS

WE TOOK ON a contractual responsibility with TCH to hire 10 percent of our workforce locally, and we set out at the beginning of the process to surpass that target.

To accomplish that goal, however, we needed a highly visible employment centre. At the time, TCH understood the importance of a physical presence and designated a retail space on Dundas adjacent to the Toronto Centre of Learning & Development.

The Regent Park Employment Centre, managed by Toronto Employment and Social Services (TESS), quickly became a celebrated model for delivering employment readiness and capacity building programs. The centre became a hub for job postings, internal to Daniels and for all our trades, suppliers, consultants, and commercial tenants. Local social service agencies also utilized the hub to connect with residents interested in joining their teams.

Under the stewardship of TESS's Georgina Elliott and subsequently Peter Foote, a small group of passionate civil servants opened doors and prepared prospective employees for success. Crystal Murphy, Fehmida Murji, and other team members provided resumé support, interview readiness training, and even access to funding for new work attire to help candidates make a positive first impression.

Over the years, fifty-five TCH residents have worked on our team, collectively earning $7,200,000 at Daniels. Beyond our direct hires, hundreds of other jobs and career path opportunities have been generated for Regent Park residents over the course of the revitalization.

Unfortunately, and against our strong advice, TESS moved out of its highly visible storefront location on Dundas into a nearly invisible new space within the new community centre at Sackville and Shuter Streets. It seemed to be a case of "out of sight, out of mind." In addition, the City's commitment to local employment initiatives and community economic development waned. It didn't take long for TESS to realize that the new location wasn't working, leaving its space within the community centre empty and forlorn.

The value of a storefront location was one of many lessons learned through the local employment initiative. We've also learned that dedicated resources are required to consistently secure job postings, build relationships with residents in search of employment opportunities, develop tracking processes, and manage those processes on an ongoing basis.

The City has a critical role within an ensemble of players implementing a robust employment strategy. Without TESS as an active participant, it became much more difficult to track outcomes and keep the band in tune.

The employment obligations of our contract were vitally important. We knew, however, that we'd have to invest significant human and financial resources well beyond our contractual requirements. Simply building new buildings wouldn't be enough. We had to learn how to build community, using the Regent Park Social Development Plan as the road map.

It was also important that our investments complement rather than duplicate work that would be led by residents, the City, TCH, and local social service agencies. With that in mind, we took a seat behind the primary players as community governance strategies were implemented, with stakeholder tables and opportunities for local residents to engage.

Recognizing gaps in what the City and TCH could achieve on their own, we jumped in with both feet, creating a "social infrastructure implementation strategy" based on three primary organizing elements:

1 Food and urban agriculture
2 Sports and recreation
3 Arts and culture

With these elements top of mind, we pushed forward, in many cases creating something from nothing. Although we led the ensemble on these initiatives, TCH's on-the-ground community development team were powerful partners.

In the early days, Lancefield Morgan was with us every step of the way, a rock-solid community builder. And then one day, TCH pulled him out. Although we were disappointed to lose Morgan, Julio Rigores stepped into the position and quickly earned a spot alongside Morgan and Barry Thomas in TCH's community builder "Hall of Fame."

VERSE TWENTY-SIX

FOOD AND URBAN AGRICULTURE

F OOD BRINGS PEOPLE TOGETHER. We knew that food would be central to our social infrastructure initiatives. Growing, cooking, eating, and sharing recipes and rituals break down barriers. With barriers removed, social cohesion has fertile ground upon which to grow.

Growing and coming together over food has a deep history in Regent Park. For decades, Blockorama, Sunday in the Park, Funky Fridays, and a host of other events brought people together, with food from around the world at the centre of each celebration. Food has also always been at the heart of the grieving process when the community comes together to mourn.

Early on, we learned that Regent Park's Sole Support Moms had created some of the first community gardens in the country, and that those gardens were a hugely important part of daily life in Regent Park.

The anger was visceral when residents learned that hundreds of garden plots would disappear because of the revitalization. Of all the issues at community meetings, the potential loss of garden plots brought the most heat. The outpouring of emotion made it very clear: we needed to design garden plots into every new rental and condominium building, while also replacing as many garden plots as possible within public spaces.

Creating the physical infrastructure within each of the new buildings was only part of the equation. Step two was to hire experts to teach the fundamentals of rooftop gardening and facilitate gardening committees in every building. Debbie Field and her team from Foodshare acted as our initial consultants, followed by Daniel Hoffmann and Jane Hayes of Hoffmann Hayes. Today, those resident committees are flourishing, with more and more people coming to understand that we *can* grow food within the urban environment.

Revisions to the phasing plan meant that the big park was going to be built within Phase Two rather than Phase Five. This was enormously impactful, providing an opportunity for the community to coalesce around the design of a critical piece of physical infrastructure in the here and now, rather than fifteen years down the road.

At the outset, the team from the City's Parks, Forestry & Recreation (PFR) division envisioned a park like every other in the city: one large open space, populated by trees and grass. However, residents spoke out loudly, demanding that the physical infrastructure deliver a foundation on which to build a strong social infrastructure. And when the residents spoke, Councillor Pam McConnell listened. With a budget facilitated by the councillor, PFR engaged hundreds of people in a robust consultation process.

It was brilliant: people of all ages participated, including TCH tenants, condominium purchasers looking forward to moving into the community, and neighbours from Cabbagetown and Corktown. All stakeholders were important voices at the design table. There were, in fact, many tables—each with ten people, on the second floor of the Regent Park South Community Centre, affectionately known as "South Centre." Each table had cut-out images of potential components of the big park, and each group was charged with building a consensus on their wish list and presenting their vision to the room. The task was to determine the must-have elements as opposed to the things that people wanted to have.

Ashrafi Ahmed, an enthusiastic community gardener and vocal critic of the loss of garden plots, began to see some positives. Perhaps the dislocation, disruption, and demolition would result in something good for everyone. In fact, the process itself was a significant turning point: the community spoke, and the city, housing company, and developer listened—a monumentally important outcome.

As a direct result, community gardens within the new park became an important ingredient. And as an indirect result, many Regent Park residents were empowered by the process. For example, Ashrafi grew into an important steward of community gardens throughout the community, working initially for the Christian Resource Centre and subsequently for Fred Victor after the two organizations merged.

In addition to community gardens, the vision that emerged included a greenhouse and bake oven with adjacent picnic tables, an off-leash dog area, playgrounds, splash pads adjacent to the Aquatic Centre, and a large outdoor field for picnics, informal play, and watching movies under the stars. Significantly, the public face of the park on Dundas Street features a grand piazza for festivities, a symbolic "welcome mat" to both local residents and people from across the city.

The big park in Regent Park is a brilliant demonstration of how a city can become an active "city-builder," harnessing and empowering local voices to bring public spaces to life. Today, for example, the bake oven is singing beautifully throughout the year. The idea was simple: create a place for people to bake and break bread together. A place to gather, with food as the currency of cohesion. What emerged is pure magic.

Presented with an opportunity to engage, people will engage. Sean Brathwaite, for example, saw the potential of establishing roots in the new Regent Park and was among the first purchasers at One Cole. Within a short time, Sean, together with a few TCH tenants and condo owners, was one of the founding members of Friends of Regent Park, which has been bringing people together at the bake oven and throughout the community for over ten years. Sean is a true community builder, teaching others how to use the bake oven, encouraging and mentoring the next generation of community leaders.

Unfortunately, the greenhouse component in the park was under-designed and under-funded, making it difficult to grow produce throughout the year. Ashrafi Ahmed and her team from Fred Victor and Sunday Harrison from Green Thumbs Growing Kids have done their best to bring the greenhouse to life in spring, summer, and fall, but are forced to shut it down over the winter.

Today, however, the team from Fred Victor is leading a discussion with Doug Bennet and Erica Roppolo of PFR about a next-gen collaboration that would ensure the greenhouse can become a year-round learning and growing hub, with a focus on food security.

PFR and Fred Victor are also working toward a refreshed management and operating agreement that would enshrine local governance and stewardship of the bake oven, greenhouse, and community gardens, putting these instruments of social cohesion into community hands, with ongoing collaboration and oversight by the city.

Cities can make it easy for grassroots organizations to flourish—or they can swamp them in red tape, with permit and fee obligations that send most groups running for the exits. Bennet, Roppolo, and the PFR team understand the exponential benefit of making it easy for local stakeholders to access physical infrastructure investments as instruments of social cohesion.

From left: Ashrafi Ahmed and Sean Brathwaite in front of the bake oven in the big park.

BRIDGE
Friends of Regent Park

Friends of Regent Park (FORP) is bringing people together throughout the year, facilitating engagement and nurturing social cohesion.

Established in August 2014, FORP is a volunteer, resident-led group that hosts events in the big park including Fall Fridays, Winterfest, Pancakes in the Park, October Funfest, skating events, community cleanups, and a weekly exercise program for older people at 252 Sackville Street.

FORP is also an active participant in Taste of Regent Park, Summer Jam, Sunday in the Park, and Party in the Park.

Friends of Regent Park brings people together in every season.

SOLO

HEELA OMARKHAIL

Heela Omarkhail has played a key leadership role in the revitalization since the very early days.

Although she was working as an administrator in support of our first condo launch, Heela's trajectory at the time was clear, with law school on the near horizon. That path took a back seat, initially for a year, when Martin Blake offered Heela a full-time role on our Regent Park team.

Heela dove into the deep trenches, working on the Phase Two and Beyond legal agreements with Martin and our stalwart team of lawyers, led by Brian Finer of Bratty & Partners.

With every nuance of the legal agreements under her belt, Heela began a deep dive into our social impact work, spearheading our social procurement initiatives, as well as the Higher Learning Initiative in partnership with the University of Toronto, her alma mater.

Heela also took charge of something we knew nothing about—running a farmers' market—determining that the best way to kick-start community engagement around food was to simply do it. In this case, just doing it meant that Heela effectively became market manager, schlepping tables, chairs, and all the fixings to Regent Park Boulevard, an investment of time and money that has generated healthy returns well into the future.

Along the way, Heela's intimate knowledge of the community led to her becoming both co-writer and co-producer of *The Journey Musical*, and more recently an onstage narrator within *Songs from The Journey*.

Today, many years from the once-intended law school path, Heela leads our social impact work across all Daniels communities.

From a bottle of Wite-Out to the Regent Park Athletic Grounds—a home for active sports and recreation.

VERSE TWENTY-SEVEN

THE SHUTER MANOEUVRE: ACTIVE SPORTS AND RECREATION

R EGENT PARK residents Amzad Khan and Tunjib Ahmed, co-founders of the Central Park Youth Sports Club, are the personification of grassroots engagement. As the revitalization began to unfold, Amzad and Tunjib witnessed high school pals caught up in the drug trade and a cycle of violence between gangs from different parts of the city.

Recognizing the importance of alternative pathways and positive role models, the two fellows started a cricket club. There was, however, one small problem: there was no place to play cricket in Regent Park. Their practices and games were in eastern Scarborough—three bus and streetcar transfers away.

When they told me this, my jaw hit the floor. Kids from Regent Park should not have to travel halfway across the city to participate in team sports. Many young athletes have the luxury of being driven to team sports by their parents. Not so in Regent Park and many other neighbourhoods across the city.

Amzad and Tunjib raised their concern at a pivotal moment—coincidental with the completion of the design process for the big park. Although a strong desire had been expressed, the park design landed with zero space for active outdoor sports.

Something needed to happen. I opened a fresh bottle of Wite-Out and began to review the master plan. Once more with feeling.

A dilapidated ice rink within Phase Three was the starting point, coupled with the all-important fact that our contract had been extended to all phases. From my initial sketches to Tom Dutton's drawing board, to Diamond Schmitt's masterful reorganization of the master plan, density was reallocated across Phase Three and a vision for the Regent Park Athletic Grounds began to emerge. Given that we didn't have buy-in from TCH or the City's planning staff, we established the "Shuter Manoeuvre" as our code name for the project.

On first review, TCH's chief development officer thought it was a terrible idea. In fact, we were told to stand down with this crazy idea. It wasn't a great moment in the history of our relationship, but we believed this was worth fighting for. Sean McIntyre, Pam McConnell's rock star constituency representative, exercised a classic piece of shuttle diplomacy. Ultimately, with the councillor on board, we convinced Len Koroneos, TCH's acting CEO at the time, that the "Shuter Manoeuvre" would create significant incremental value for TCH and the entire community.

Koroneos's response was crystal clear: *if* we didn't lose a single square foot of density, and *if* we could find a path to paying for it, we would jump into the deep end together and make it happen.

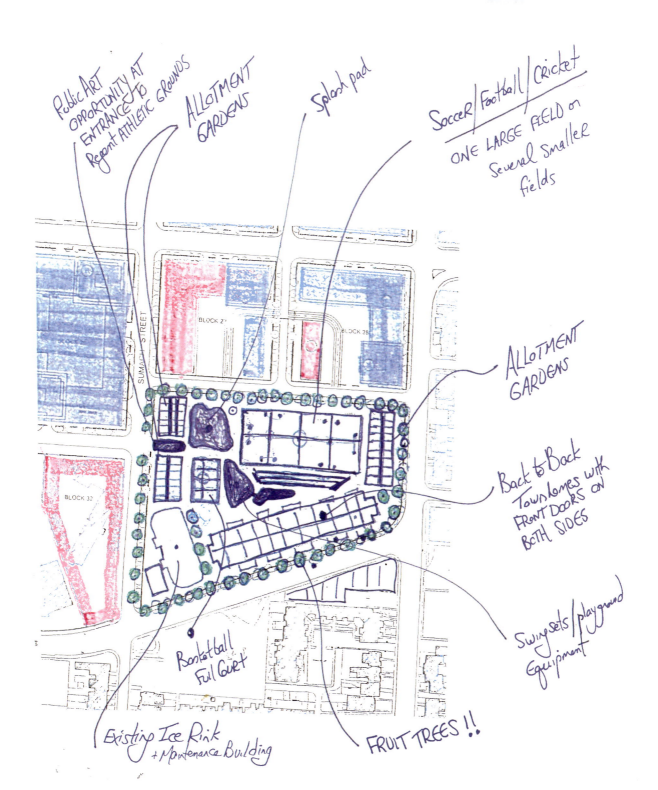

That's what developers do. Jump in. Make things happen.

In short order, Remo Agostino, now our chief development officer, brought city planning on board. Lucky Boothe of the City's PFR department gave an enthusiastic thumbs-up, and Kenneth Slater and the team from Dixon Hall became active facilitators, engaging local residents in the design as well as envisioning how this new physical infrastructure would be programmed to facilitate social cohesion.

Finding the money was as important as getting everyone on side. The options were twofold: door number one was a capital campaign similar to the Daniels Spectrum fundraising effort. Alternatively, door number two was to find a single donor to "own" the opportunity.

This was the preferred route, with one obvious door on which to knock: Maple Leaf Sports & Entertainment (MLSE). A call to Ken Tanenbaum led to a meeting with the CEO of the MLSE Foundation.

After singing and dancing our way through why our idea should be a no-brainer for MLSE, the Foundation's CEO gave us a firm thumbs-down. In short, the Foundation was providing cash contributions averaging

$25,000 to schools and community organizations to refurbish ancient basketball courts. Our proposal was nowhere near a fit.

Later, when MLSE Foundation appointed a new acting CEO, I requested a further kick at the proverbial can. Once again we sang and danced, but we received a second thumbs-down.

A few months later, the clouds miraculously parted, sunshine engulfed the Presentation Centre, and Mike Bartlett, then new CEO of MLSE Foundation, walked in the door. Bartlett got it, big time: an opportunity for the Foundation to be fully engaged in community, not with a one-time contribution but with a long-term relationship.

With fire in his eyes, Bartlett went to his board and achieved a commitment that the Foundation would raise $3 million: $2 million would be allocated for physical infrastructure, and $1 million would go to supporting a "participatory grant-making" program over the first five years. For our part, we committed to building the Athletic Grounds at cost, waiving construction management fees.

MLSE's monumental pledge opened the door to physical infrastructure that supported health and well-being while providing a myriad of opportunities for social infrastructure to take root. Their approach to participatory grant-making was also a breakthrough, demonstrating how engagement philanthropy and collective action can have an exponential impact on the health and well-being of a community.

TCH's two conditions had been fulfilled. First, density had been redistributed, and in fact increased, through a Phase Three rezoning. And second, with the lion's share of funding brought to the table by MLSE Foundation, additional value was created for all stakeholders.

A big win for everyone.

BRIDGE
Bones of Contention

Our initial proposal was for TCH to enter into a licence agreement with Dixon Hall for operation, maintenance, and programming of the Athletic Grounds. Unfortunately, despite all our best arguments, community stewardship wasn't in the cards.

Perpetually strapped for cash, the City wanted to own and generate income from the Athletic Grounds, leasing it to soccer and other leagues from across the city.

With cash as the driver, TCH transferred ownership to the City, which delegated operations to Parks, Forestry & Recreation (PFR). As a result, the local community has felt short-changed over the years, with limited affordable access, since MLSE's granting pool has been depleted.

Access to the Pam McConnell Aquatic Centre has also been a significant bone of contention for local residents. PFR's registration systems are digital and rely on people owning a computer, knowing how to navigate a registration system, and having the time to log on at the precise moment the portal opens.

VERSE TWENTY-EIGHT

ARTS AND CULTURE

T HE FIRST STEP OF THE REVITALIZATION was physical—putting the streets back in, correcting one of the fundamental flaws of the "garden city" model. The next step was to create reasons for people from outside to stop inside and hang out.

Arts and culture, our third primary organizing element, was that next step, and we began envisioning ways to make Regent Park a go-to destination rather than a place to avoid.

One pathway emerged as I listened to Matt Galloway on CBC's *Metro Morning* interviewing Marjan Verstappen and Humboldt Magnussen, founders of Younger Than Beyoncé (YTB), a nomadic DIY art gallery for emergent and experimental artists. It was happenstance that I was listening at the moment Marjan said that YTB was looking for their first pop-up space. I emailed Matt, who connected me to Marjan and Humboldt. Within a few weeks, YTB had moved into Regent Park, bringing the coolest artists, curators, and creators into the community for the first time.

At around the same time, a gift from the heavens landed on our doorstep in the form of internationally recognized choreographers Laurence

Lemieux and Bill Coleman. Lemieux and Coleman decided to leave their studio in Montreal and create a new home for their creative energies in Toronto. Their work was about dance, but much more than that too. It was also large-scale, interactive, off-the-beaten-track cultural experiences in Newfoundland, Mongolia, and other far-flung regions of the world.

To our immense good fortune, they bought the long-neglected Citadel building at 304 Parliament Street, directly across from Regent Park. The Citadel, built in 1912 and then most recently owned by the Salvation Army, was in desperate need of both tender loving care and a vision. Lemieux and Coleman brought both to the building and the neighbourhood.

An indomitable spirit of adventure flowed from the two choreographers, energizing everyone to make the Citadel an important artistic hub. Diamond Schmitt Architects came on board, with Don Schmitt and team contributing hundreds of pro bono hours. Step by step, the Citadel: Ross Centre for Dance was created, with significant support from Gretchen and Donald Ross.

I heard about our new neighbours in spring 2009. Naturally neighbourly and inquisitive, I knocked on their door and was bowled over by their desire to become an active partner in the revitalization. It was a match made in artistic heaven. Our goal was to put Regent Park on the map artistically, enabling people to conjure images other than that of a neighbourhood to avoid. Lemieux and Coleman were ready, willing, able, and enthusiastic about helping us achieve that goal.

Coleman Lemieux & Compagnie's spectacular rain-soaked production of *On Broken Ground*.

VERSE TWENTY-NINE

SHOWTIME

IT WAS POURING RAIN all day and into the evening of Friday, July 24, 2009, the night before showtime for our first collaboration. This was going to be an important milestone—a calling card to the world: Regent Park is changing.

Heather Ogden of the National Ballet and a host of other artists, including actor Jackie Burroughs, were part of the show. Our heavy-machine operators were poised to make their backhoes dance as a backdrop for *On Broken Ground*, a performance art piece celebrating rebirth—a literal and figurative coming "from the ground."

The entire community had been invited, as were our recent purchasers at One Cole. Our goal was to reinforce their purchase decision, energizing our early adopters to become word-of-mouth ambassadors for the transformation.

There was a lot at stake. And the rain didn't look like it was going to stop. I lost my nerve and called Bill Coleman on Friday evening.

"Bill, it's Mitchell. I'd like to postpone the event. Let's call it off now and alert everyone that we're postponing for a week."

"Mitchell... no way, not a chance... please trust me on this. The rain will make it *so* much better. It will be spectacular."

Bill was right. It was spectacular.

BRIDGE
Showtime: Take Two

Less than a year later, *The New World*, a second performance art extravaganza, was equally magical. Hundreds of people participated in a performance that stretched across all of Phase One. Coleman Lemieux & Compagnie engaged firefighters, police officers, marching bands, construction workers, and residents of all ages to be part of the show.

The City closed Parliament Street on that momentous day as we celebrated the opening of Cole Street, the first public street in Regent Park in over fifty years. Jackie Richardson and the Tynes Family Singers performed "Dancing Down the Avenue" as we literally, in that instant, reconnected Regent Park with the rest of the world.

"DANCING DOWN THE AVENUE" from *The Journey Musical*

Hello Oak Street, here's to Pat Cole, here's to a place with a whole lotta soul:

A long time ago, they closed them down, thought it was the right thing to do.
Who was to know it, how we could blow it, taking out the avenues.

Years gone by, we've learned a thing or two, about front doors right on the street.
It all comes round, what's old is new, on the street, that's where we'll meet.

Now we're dancing down the avenue, dancing down the avenue.

I do my banking, it isn't a chore, never had a local bank before.
Having coffee at Tims is a treat, the folks that run it live right up the street.
Dad calls for a pizza, it comes to my door, that ain't the way it used to be before.
Don't have to cab it from the grocery store, this is the way it should be...
Now we're dancing down the avenue, dancing down the avenue.

Now we're dancing down the avenue, dancing down the avenue.

VERSE THIRTY

ENVISIONING AN ARTS AND CULTURAL CENTRE

THE SOCIAL DEVELOPMENT PLAN (SDP) made it clear: the "new" Regent Park *must* include a place where people from all cultures could share and showcase their art, music, dance, theatre, and spoken word. Although the SDP contemplated a theoretical arts and cultural centre, neither the zoning bylaw nor the original concept plan included this important use.

The fundamental disconnect was painfully obvious, and we took on the challenge of connecting the theoretical with the real. The Phase Two and Beyond contract allowed us to step into the void.

It began with another bottle of Wite-Out: I pressed my primary architectural design tool into service to envision a cultural centre deliberately positioned in the heart of the community.

Tom Dutton and Remo Agostino, our vice president of development, along with Diamond Schmitt Architects, took my messy sketch and turned it into a rezoning application for Phase Two, moving residential densities from that central zone to other buildings in proximity. Most importantly, we demonstrated to our partner that no density would be lost. We also voiced the strong opinion that additional value would be created if an arts and cultural centre could be manifested in the heart of the community.

    An initial visioning process was facilitated by Lord Cultural Resources. A second and deeper dive was required to build a case for support, and Toronto Artscape Inc. was contracted to facilitate an engagement process that included local residents of all ages, social service agencies, and arts advocates from across the city. Under CEO Tim Jones's leadership, Artscape's Pru Robey, Reid Henry, and Billie Bridgeman worked with all stakeholders, setting the table for what was about to unfold. This was my introduction to Tim Jones, who for years had been building Artscape into a powerful force within the local and global arts community.

    Many arts organizations look at developers as the devil incarnate, often for good reason. The gentrification cycle is well documented and has repeated itself in cities across North America and beyond. First, artists migrate to affordable spaces in derelict neighbourhoods. Second, over time, those neighbourhoods become the centre of cool and eventually too expensive for artists to remain. Next, developers squeeze out all remaining tenants with exorbitant rent increases. The goal: wipe out the old and bring in shiny new towers with zero affordable spaces for artists to live or work.

    Jones understood the cycle but was determined to turn it on its head, embracing development as an opportunity, rather than a curse. In fact, Jones firmly believed that enormous value can be created for artists, local communities, and all stakeholders at the intersection of business and the arts.

Our TIFF Bell Lightbox experience in Toronto's entertainment district certainly reinforced that belief. In that case, we stood at one side of the intersection with *Ghostbusters* director and producer Ivan Reitman and his sisters Agi Mandel and Susan Michaels. On the other side was the Toronto International Film Festival Group, intent on creating a new destination for film lovers from around the world. We met in the middle, and the result was a cultural institution that has brought hundreds of millions of dollars of value to the city, while nurturing filmmakers and creators of all ages and backgrounds.

With that in mind, TCH and Daniels initiated a request for proposal process to identify an organization that would help create and subsequently manage an arts and cultural centre in the heart of Regent Park. Artscape and one other proponent responded, and Artscape was contracted to turn the dream into reality.

This was no easy task: How could a new cultural centre reflect the local community while also breaking down barriers separating Regent Park from the rest of the city? What was the best legal structure? Who should own the new facility, and how should it be governed?

With Celia Smith, Artscape's CEO, on lead guitar, it didn't take long for a powerful framework to emerge, one that has stood the test of time.

Everything starts with a piece of land, and TCH's leadership team rose to the occasion, providing a fifty-year land lease for one dollar to Regent Park Arts Non-Profit Development Corporation (RPAD), a new single-purpose entity. This was a hugely important building block of the cross-sectoral collaboration that created Daniels Spectrum.

Smith described the collaboration as a four-legged stool that wouldn't have survived without each leg supporting, listening, and respecting what the others brought to the equation. In Smith's recollection, each leg of the stool had its own character: TCH was the elephant—a behemoth of an organization that had never envisioned, built, or even thought about creating a cultural centre as a "value creation" opportunity. Daniels was the tiger—driving timely decision making and tirelessly looking for new partners to bring to the table. Artscape was the mouse, the new kid on the block, trying to navigate positive outcomes for everyone but most importantly for residents—who were the critical fourth leg of the stool.

Despite the different frameworks from which each of the collaborators emerged, each leg supported and provided strength to the others. With a piece of a land, an operational framework, and all four legs dancing in syncopated rhythm, we were ready to rock and roll.

We also generated insight through extensive community consultation, including from potential anchor tenants. Leslie Lester of Soulpepper Theatre Company provided invaluable input into must-have design elements, including a flexible black box event and performance space that could be used for every possible iteration of a show, gala, or community gathering.

With that important information, Donald Schmitt and Jennifer Mallard of Diamond Schmitt Architects translated the initial vision into an architectural expression that has not only generated numerous design awards, but also provided a springboard for building social cohesion, a veritable "community living room," welcoming and open to everyone.

BRIDGE

Withstanding the Challenges of COVID-19

The COVID years were particularly challenging to the ecosystem of artists and arts organizations across the country. Artscape was no exception. With many tenants unable to pay rent and zero revenue from what had been a robust events business, Artscape was forced into a receivership process at the end of August 2023, requiring the sale of some of its assets.

The local ownership framework created for Regent Park's new arts and culture centre ensured that it was immune to the receivership process, allowing RPAD and Daniels Spectrum to maintain continuous operations throughout and beyond the receivership.

VERSE THIRTY-ONE

FUNDING AN ARTS AND CULTURAL CENTRE

DEVELOPING A VISION and operational framework is one thing. Finding cash to build the vision is another matter altogether. Although the economic meltdown in 2008 had many damaging side effects, one upside was the creation of the Federal Infrastructure Stimulus Fund. The intent was to stimulate construction of roads, sewers, bridges, and transit lines across the province, with municipalities creating lists of priority projects. Although Toronto had a long list of priorities, an arts and cultural centre was *not* one of them—at least, until it was.

Enter Robert Foster, chair of Artscape, who initiated an arm-twisting campaign that spelled out the importance of this investment to the future of the overall revitalization. Foster, a supernatural force bridging the business and cultural communities, worked magic with MP John Baird in Ottawa and MPP George Smitherman at Queen's Park, convincing both fellows that a cultural hub was an infrastructure investment that would generate positive social returns for generations to come.

With both levels of government on side, the final decision rested with the City. It was a Hail Mary moment when at the very last minute Robert Foster and Tim Jones convinced Mayor David Miller to add this critical investment to Toronto's priority list.

The result: the federal and provincial governments each committed $12 million, augmenting the City's land contribution with most of the cash required to build the new facility.

With $24 million in hand, Foster along with philanthropist Judy Matthews and a small but mighty campaign cabinet settled into biweekly breakfast meetings at our presentation centre to raise the balance. Cathy Ciccolini, Anthony Ciccolini, Ralph Lean, Thomas Gerginis, and the City's Lori Martin joined me at the cabinet table with Foster and Matthews. (One of the highlights of our meetings were the cannoli that the Ciccolinis brought in from Woodbridge. With that taste of heaven coursing through our veins, there was no doubt the campaign would be successful!)

Our team at Daniels committed $500,000 to kick-start the campaign with a Tenant Transition Fund that would ensure rents would be affordable for non-profit organizations making the leap into a new home.

An anonymous donor contributed $1.25 million, and philanthropist Gary Slaight came to the table to name the main performance hall after his mother, Ada. Slaight also contributed his mom's beautiful piano, which is still being played for special events in Ada Slaight Hall.

Jones and Foster secured a naming donor with a $4 million pledge. Three months before opening day, however, that donor was spooked by Sue-Ann Levy's *Toronto Sun* stories and pulled the plug on their pledge. Within twenty-four hours, we committed to replace the runaway donor with $2 million from the John and Myrna Daniels Charitable Foundation and $2 million from The Daniels Corporation. In hindsight, we should have stepped up as naming donor on day one, but when the opportunity came back around, we were thrilled to seize the moment.

Opening celebrations kicked off in September 2012 with CBC's Matt Galloway broadcasting *Metro Morning* from just outside the east doors of the Spectrum. Joan Melanson, *Metro Morning*'s executive producer, had arranged a few special guests for the show, including Mustafa Ahmed, a young man whose powerful spoken-word poetry was resonating with young people in Regent Park and throughout the city.

It was a monumental moment: the ears of the entire city were tuned into Regent Park, with an open invitation to visit Daniels Spectrum, the physical infrastructure that would support the evolution of a healthy social infrastructure for decades to come.

Twelve years after opening its doors for the first time, the building continues to be true to its tagline: "Rooted in Regent Park, Open to the World." From a bottle of Wite-Out in 2009 to doors open in 2012—a brilliantly successful part of the journey.

BRIDGE
Bringing Anchor Tenants to the New Cultural Centre

A small colourful sign on a tiny townhome on Queen Street near Sumach tipped me off: RPSM—the Regent Park School of Music. I thought, *Something very cool must be happening inside.*

One day in 2005, as part of our "listen and learn" tour, I knocked on the door and discovered a world of music: a student drummer and a teacher banging away in the basement, a chorus of singers in the living room. An admin team member was in the kitchen. Every bedroom on the second and third floors was flush with teachers and kids from Regent Park learning the language of music. Two hundred young smiling faces, ages four to eighteen, were receiving free or "pay what you can" music lessons.

Over the next few years, I spent time in that small but brilliant space getting to know the management team as well as Tom Kennedy, Stan Witkin, Louise Sugar, and other board members led by chair Jill Witkin. It was a tough decision, but the board took a leap into the unknown and committed to creating a significantly expanded home for the school within the new cultural centre.

This was momentous, signalling faith that a local grassroots organization was willing to build a platform for growth and sustainability within the heart of the revitalization.

Richard Marsella led RPSM's evolution from Queen Street into its new home and has made magic ever since. Under Marsella's stewardship, some of the world's foremost artists, including Roger Waters, Jully Black, Broken Social Scene, and even Taylor Swift, have collaborated with kids from Regent Park. Marsella even convinced iconic jazz ensemble Sun Ra Arkestra to perform at Spectrum's grand opening in 2012 and welcomed them back to celebrate Spectrum's tenth anniversary.

With RPSM setting up shop within the new arts and cultural centre, other groups followed, including the Regent Park Film Festival. The festival remains one of the only free film festivals in the city and has risen to the upper echelon of Toronto's go-to events. It has also become a much-loved local institution, hosting free films under the stars over the summer in the big park.

Similarly, ArtHeart Community Art Centre, founded in 1991 and passionately guided over the decades by Seanna Connell, Sandi Wong, and Timothy Svirklys, climbed out of a church basement at Dundas and Sackville Streets into the vibrant second floor at Daniels Spectrum. Pathways to Education, a "made in Regent Park" mentorship program, also committed to space within the new centre, as did the Collective of Black Artists (COBA), which moved into Regent Park from its home in the West End.

Native Earth Performing Arts (NEPA) created Aki Studio to showcase Indigenous theatre on the ground floor and established its centre of operations on the second floor.

Tonya Surman and her team from the Centre for Social Innovation established CSI Regent Park on the third floor, bringing a host of social entrepreneurs and enterprise businesses together. Under Denise Soueidan-O'Leary's leadership, CSI Regent Park was a rock-solid community partner both within and beyond Daniels Spectrum, working tirelessly to build community wealth and a healthy social infrastructure.

A recent addition to the second floor at Spectrum is The Children's Book Bank. Founder and then executive director Kim Beatty created a cozy home for the book bank just outside the footprint of Regent Park. Ten years later, with a landlord threatening to push them out, Kim's successor, Mary Ladky, brought the book bank to Daniels Spectrum, adding children's literacy to the many strands of arts, culture, and community resonating throughout the building.

Today, Daniels Spectrum is home to seventeen arts-based, learning, and community-focussed organizations and a destination for thousands of visitors to Regent Park.

SET FIVE

A FUSION OF MELODIES

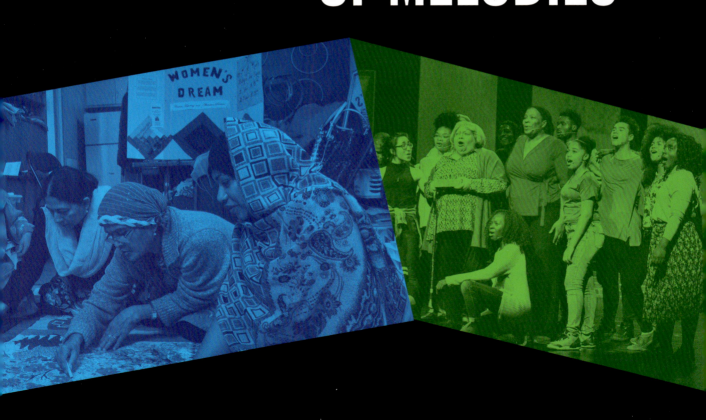

VERSE THIRTY-TWO

THE JOURNEY MUSICAL

As the transformation moved forward, I also continued my musical journey, co-writing several songs with Henry Heillig, some of which you've seen in this book, including "Dancing Down the Avenue" and "Show Love."

However, it was "Under One Roof," a song commemorating the opening of Daniels Spectrum, that opened the door to something larger—a realization that the individual songs could become much more.

A lightning bolt of a revelation hit me on February 6, 2013, as Janice and I were flying home from London. I had been invited by Pavi Binning of George Weston Limited and the Prince's Trust to join a delegation visiting Prince Charles (now king). We had tea, biscuits, formalities, and lively conversation at Clarence House as guests of His Royal Highness, a memorable moment for a boy from Regina.

As we reached cruising altitude on the flight home, I opened my laptop, and somehow it became instantly clear that the songs we'd written, combined with other song and story ideas that had been percolating, could become a full-blown musical.

In that eureka moment, I also recognized an opportunity to combine a lifelong love of music and songwriting with a passion for building community. In fact, by the time we landed, I had written a first draft of the musical as well as the bones of a plan by which the musical would exponentially expand our community development toolbox.

Four songs became six, six became ten, interwoven with stories that looked back at the history of the community as well as real-time challenges and opportunities of the revitalization.

Heela Omarkhail came on board as co-writer and co-producer, embracing the musical as a unique opportunity to further our impact work. Together, we reached out to local stakeholders, both young and old, with a view to ensuring we got it right—or as close to right as possible.

As outsiders, it was essential to be super-sensitive to nuance, to getting the stories right, reflecting the challenges while also portraying a glimmer of hope for the future. Most importantly, we couldn't whitewash the past or sugar-coat the dislocation and disruption of the present. We also had to bring immediate value to the community.

With that in mind, *The Journey Musical* became a vehicle to support youth arts programming and capital repairs within Daniels Spectrum. Perhaps most importantly, net proceeds from the musical would ensure that rents for anchor tenants would remain affordable.

Our strategy was simple: knock on the door of every company that had thus far touched the revitalization. The response was extraordinary. Electricians, plumbers, drywall contractors, banks, insurance providers, architects, engineers, post-secondary institutions... everyone came to the table, inspired by the opportunity to contribute to the social, cultural, and economic evolution of the community.

Wayne London, CEO of concrete supplier Innocon, grabbed the presenting sponsorship opportunity, and his successor, David Redfern, maintained that leadership role through each successive production.

Artscape shared the load on production logistics and fundraising through Toronto Artscape Foundation. Over the years, Leslie Najgebauer, Jane Hopgood, Brooke Duvall, Elaina Pawelka, and the entire Artscape team were powerful co-producers and partners.

Raising funds was one part of the equation. The other was to be strategic on the expenditure side. Social procurement and local economic impact became fundamental building blocks for every aspect of each production.

To that end, local social enterprises, including Infinigard and Coat Check 4 Change, were contracted for security and coat check services, and caterers from the Regent Park Catering Collective provided a delicious meal in advance of each community presentation. Local artists and arts organizations, including ArtHeart, designed decor for the gala presentations.

On the artistic side, casting young people from the neighbourhood as actors, singers, dancers, and spoken-word artists was top-line important, with additional mentorships for set design, photography, and every possible component of the show.

Trevlyn Kennedy, Limees Rizeig, Britta B., Steve Harmony, Stacy Darko, Charlotte Siegel, Jael Jones Cabey, Masima Lawrence, Bradley Smart, and a host of other young people from the neighbourhood were part of a large ensemble cast.

Professionals performed alongside the young performers. Jackie Richardson, a Canadian musical icon, played granny to kids from the neighbourhood, delivering big-time from the first table read to the final curtain call, demonstrating the focus and energy required to deliver a professional performance. Actor and singer Alana Bridgewater played a key role in each production, mentoring the young performers along with Jeremiah Sparks, Gavin Hope, Quisha Wint, Sterling Jarvis, Karen Jewels, and other Canadian theatre veterans.

The Journey Orchestra rocked the casbah: Henry Heillig, co-writer and music director, played bass, and Charlie Cooley laid it down on drums and percussion—an incomparable rhythm section. Guitar virtuoso Eric St-Laurent along with Alison Young on saxophones and keyboardists Stacie McGregor and Thompson Egbo-Egbo rounded out the orchestra.

It was especially wonderful to have Egbo-Egbo on the team. His family arrived in Canada from Nigeria and settled in Regent Park when he was four years old. Dixon Hall Music School was the first step on his musical journey, followed by jazz performance studies at Humber College and subsequently the Berklee College of Music in Boston.

We were confident that our gala audience would be appreciative. The true test was how folks from the community would react to "outsiders" telling their story. With fingernails chewed to the bone, we took the stage for our first community performance. Would we, could we, hit the right chord?

We got our answer in the form of a standing ovation with stamping feet and a lot of hooting and hollering. It was deeply moving to know that our friends in the community felt good about how the story of their lives was being told.

Over the years, *The Journey Musical* has had incredible directors leading both the cast and production crew. Anne-Marie Woods directed the first two productions, and Kate Fenton the second two, with Apolonia Velasquez and Ofilio Portillo from Gadfly choreographing each of the four shows. Laurence Lemieux choreographed "Quilt of Love," a deeply emotional moment within each of the productions.

Mitchell (centre) and the cast bringing energy and unity to the stage, singing and dancing to "Under One Roof" during the *Songs from The Journey* performance at Koerner Hall.

VERSE THIRTY-THREE

MEMORABLE MOMENTS FROM *THE JOURNEY MUSICAL*

Producing the musical delivered many highs and lows... including moments of extreme panic.

Some of the challenges we brought on ourselves, including the decision to create Moze Mossanen's documentary *My Piece of the City*. The film, produced by Teresa Ho of 100 Dragons Media, premiered at TIFF Bell Lightbox and subsequently opened the Regent Park Film Festival in 2017.

The stress levels were through the roof throughout the 2016 rehearsal process. Mossanen was sensitive to the challenges but also keen to have cameras rolling and microphones hot through every rehearsal, leading to a few super-tense moments but which also resulted in a deeply moving story.

This was also the production in which I had to fire a young performer following dress rehearsal, a few hours before showtime.

Another low point and unforgettable jolt to the system came partway through that same 2016 production. The phone rang at my Daniels office at 4 p.m. on a Friday, a few hours before the evening show. It was Kenneth

Slater calling to let me know that the police would be lying in wait at the Spectrum to arrest one of our young stars before the show.

Kenneth and I met the fine folks from 51 Division in the soundproof screening room at the Regent Park Film Festival and ultimately convinced them that "the show must go on." That was, however, coupled with a solemn promise that the young man would turn himself in on Sunday morning, which allowed him to be in our closing performance on Saturday night.

As "Under One Roof" was closing the last act, Kenneth tiptoed down from the balcony, tapped me on the shoulder, and gestured emphatically for me to follow him. The look on his face spelled TROUBLE in capital letters.

My heart sank. I held my breath. The brilliant euphoria of the last song was punctured by my certainty that the young man had been shot for real after having been theatrically shot onstage a few minutes earlier.

And then—an enormous sigh of relief when I found out he hadn't been shot. Instead, the young man had literally exited stage left and disappeared out the back door into the night. Although he didn't show up at 51 Division in the morning, Kenneth was able to track him down and got him there by 5 p.m. that day.

Over the years, we had all come a long way on the journey of the revitalization. And when COVID led to the cancellation of the production scheduled for June 2020, I came to the conclusion that the curtain had come down for good on *The Journey Musical*.

But then, in July 2022, local residents Murwan Khogali and Ines Garcia sat me down at a community event and told me in no uncertain terms, "You must bring back *The Journey*." I canvassed other friends in the neighbourhood. Yasin, Lloyd, Marlene, and many others echoed that initial refrain: "Bring back *The Journey*."

Songs from The Journey evolved from those discussions. With Apolonia Velasquez in the director's chair, this "greatest hits" version of *The Journey Musical* was first performed at Daniels Spectrum in November 2022.

When the curtain came down on that production, that same group of friends implored us to take the story beyond the confines of their neighbourhood. They believed, as we do, that their story of grit and resilience, determination and transformation, was worth telling a broader audience, which took us to the magnificent Koerner Hall in June 2024.

Over the years, four iterations of *The Journey Musical: A Living History of the Regent Park Revitalization* and two productions of *Songs from The Journey* have raised over $5 million to support youth arts programming, capital repairs, and the tenant sustainability fund at Daniels Spectrum.

The most recent production at Koerner Hall also kick-started the My Piece of the City program, enabling the Royal Conservatory of Music to augment affordable access to Koerner Hall for Toronto's diverse cultural communities.

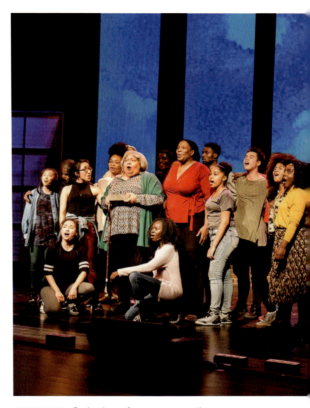

 Grab a box of popcorn, scan the QR code, and enjoy Moze Mossanen's compelling documentary of the revitalization story through the eyes of our performers as they rehearsed for the 2016 production of *The Journey*.

VERSE THIRTY-FOUR

A BALANCING ACT

Although the history is still being written, the Regent Park revitalization is looked at by many as the gold standard by which a challenged inner-city neighbourhood can be reimagined and transformed. Others feel that we should have pushed harder to achieve better outcomes on a number of fronts.

It has been a balancing act on many levels, with a myriad of decisions and conflicting opinions and interests to consider. Some decisions were ours to make. Others we had no say in whatsoever, but we still did our best to influence the decision makers, whether at TCH or the City.

One of the substantive issues was whether one or more of the mid-century Peter Dickinson buildings in South Regent Park should be preserved.

There was never doubt that Toronto's traditional grid system of streets and an interconnected public realm of sidewalks and crosswalks should be reinstated, with a public-facing park connecting north, south, east, and west. Within that framework, Ken Greenberg, John Gladki, Ronji Borooah, and others, alongside TCH, looked at tower locations and density disposition with a view to creating a walkable community with wide sidewalks and a generous public realm. Successive rezonings added both density and new public infrastructure, including Daniels Spectrum and the Regent Park Athletic Grounds. Significantly, these new approvals were accomplished within the existing framework, adding a few stories to each of the towers while maintaining tower separation and podiums with "activation" retail along both Parliament and Dundas Streets.

The new grid, which simply reintroduced the pre–garden city grid, was malleable, allowing the plan to evolve naturally as new opportunities emerged. Greenberg often reflects on this malleability as a primary lesson learned from the process.

Over the years, nineteen architectural firms have manifested designs within the grid framework, creating streets and a pedestrian experience that are at once fresh and wholly recognizable, comfortable places to walk, live, play, and experience life. (See Coda for the full compendium of architectural firms, along with photos of their creations.)

Some large-scale master plan developments are prioritizing "starchitects" to bring a wow factor. In our view, each of the architectural firms that have touched Regent Park is a star. Each has created a building or buildings that listen to and respect each other, that are both beautiful and rational, creating a context in which community happens. Everywhere.

There is, however, significant disagreement about the Dickinson buildings. Many preservationists believe that one or more should have been saved. In short, the critique is that our public/private partnership should have been more creative in saving and generating an adaptive new use for at least one of the Dickinson buildings.

One vociferous argument on the other side of the ledger came from TCH tenants, who made it clear that, regardless of architectural merit, these buildings symbolized the worst of government housing and needed to be torn down for Regent Park to truly emerge as a revitalized community.

The Dickinson buildings were designed to demonstrate that large families could live happily in two-storey units within a fourteen-storey tower.

The skip-corridor design resulted in unsupervised stairwells, uninterrupted by corridors for two floors. It didn't take long for these isolated stairwell spaces to become the exclusive purview of drug dealers and users. Tragically, given how often elevators were broken down, kids were forced to navigate these stairwells on their way to and from school. All too often, those stairwells were populated with condoms, empty syringes, and victims of overnight overdoses.

Globe and Mail journalist John Bentley Mays, lamenting the potential loss of the "Dickinsons," solicited adaptive reuse ideas from his readers in March 2013. Any one of the ideas could have been implemented if two things had come together: boatloads of money falling from heaven and an owner with zero concern about breaking even on a business plan, let alone making a nickel.

One suggestion was to turn one of the buildings into a hotel—a total non-starter. Another was to create a multi-storey electrified farmers' market. A "bright" idea, indeed—but totally impossible.

Highly respected Toronto architect and affordable housing innovator John van Nostrand and his colleague Pat Hansen had done a condo conversion workup in 2005 and postulated in the Bentley Mays article that a "retrofit to condo" was a viable option.

Our team did a thorough analysis and concluded we would never recoup our investment. Martin Blake and I laid it out to van Nostrand and his colleague Drew Sinclair at Paintbox Bistro. Environmental remediation alone, including asbestos removal, significantly added to the risk and cost of adaptive reuse. Perhaps another developer would have been prepared to take that risk. We weren't.

We also believed that the grid-based master plan proposed throughout all phases was a significant improvement over leaving this remnant of the "garden city." Walking the streets of South Regent today reinforces that belief.

Practical reality has butted heads with unbridled idealism on many occasions throughout the process. In this case, and on balance, we believed the Dickinsons had to go.

We did, however, commission Cal Brook and the team from Brook McIlroy to develop an adaptive reuse plan for Regent Park's district energy plant, including the tall brick smokestack, a focal point and vista termination at the north end of the big park. Our adaptive reuse proposal combined a new 25,000-square-foot Toronto Public Library (TPL) connected to program space within the energy plant building.

The Brook McIlroy plan totally rocked. Within days, we had Councillor Pam McConnell's blessing, as well as a $16.3 million funding allocation spearheaded by TPL's Vickery Bowles and Moe Hosseini-Ara.

Sadly, Pam McConnell wasn't able to steward this dream to reality. In our last meeting, six weeks before she passed away, Pam took my hands in hers, looked me in the eye, and asked me to promise that I would make the dream of a new library come true. Leaving that promise unfulfilled is one of my biggest regrets.

We hope this adaptive reuse concept, integrated with a new library, will become a reality as part of the Phases Four and Five plan. However, we no longer have a voice at that table.

SOLO

A TRIBUTE TO PAM MCCONNELL

I wrote the following tribute shortly after Pam passed away in early summer 2017.

> I have been blessed to have known and been inspired by Pam McConnell since 1980. In fact, I'll never forget our first encounter.
>
> I was the newbie at Co-op Housing Federation of Toronto, and Pam was chair of the board, leading a group of passionate progressive people who were not just dreaming big dreams but also literally building the co-op housing movement across the country.
>
> I was on my way to observe my first board meeting. Pam stopped me in the hallway, grabbed both my arms, and in thirty seconds or less welcomed me to CHFT and told me that co-op housing was going to empower tenants across the country, and that together we were going to build a better world. And then with a big smile and twinkle in her eye, she spun around and was gone.
>
> I stood there in shock, electrified by a single moment with this small but enormously powerful woman.
>
> Pam's leadership in building and supporting the co-op housing movement

across the country has positively impacted thousands upon thousands of lives. Today, however, I'm here to speak about the Pam McConnell that I had the honour of working with in Regent Park over the past eleven years.

There were many memorable moments over those years, but the one that stands out, the one I'll always remember, is when we met after our company entered a partnership with Toronto Community Housing on the Regent Park revitalization.

In that meeting, Pam delivered a detailed history lesson on the Regent Park community, on the grassroots origins of the revitalization, on the zoning bylaw for the entire sixty-nine acres that she had shepherded through council, and on the importance of building social infrastructure for the new community that would be as strong as the new bricks and mortar.

At the end of the conversation, Pam put it very simply... she said... Mitchell... above all else we need to honour and respect the residents. If we do that, we can make this work.

Today, there is no doubt that Pam lived and breathed honour and respect for the residents of Regent Park. And she fought for residents every step of the way, creating the big park fifteen years ahead of the original schedule, building the Aquatic Centre, the Athletic Grounds, and the community centre, creating the physical assets around which the social infrastructure she envisioned could flourish.

Pam's vision for the revitalization was clear, and her passion to get it right ran deep. In short, there is no doubt that without Pam McConnell, there wouldn't be a Regent Park revitalization.

Pam was there from minute one, not just dreaming big dreams but doing the heavy lifting to bring those dreams to life. Pam has been both the glue and the common thread, the unifying and trusted voice, holding steady to the vision despite a myriad of obstacles along the path.

Although the residents of Regent Park have lost their champion, Pam's voice and vision will live on...

"FROM THE ROOFTOPS" from *The Journey Musical*
A tribute to Pam McConnell first performed in 2018

There was always a place at your table, always room in your tent.
When everybody gathered, everybody mattered, you inspired wherever you went.

We'll never forget you, never let you go, won't forget the smile in your eye.
A lifetime of caring, a lifetime of sharing, always fighting for the little guy.

From the rooftops, from the rooftops, everybody's singing,
Singing songs of love to you.
From the rooftops, from the rooftops, all across the city
Singing songs of love to you…

We're tending to your roses, pulling every weed, breaking bread and sharing every bowl.
You started something we're bound to carry on, from deep in your heart and soul…

And we will carry on, carry on, carry on with songs of love for you…
About your coat of many colours, your care for many others, songs of love for you.
About the children, your children, our children, songs of love for you.
And we will carry on, carry on, carry on, with songs of love for you.

VERSE THIRTY-FIVE

AN EVOLUTION IN PHILANTHROPIC THINKING

Over the years, there has been considerable dialogue about the impact and root causes of gun violence in the neighbourhood. The daytime shooting at the Eaton Centre in June 2012 stimulated these important discussions.

One part of the conversation centred on how to help family members cope with the trauma. Another was to develop early intervention strategies that would change the trajectory for as many young people as possible.

We were invited to participate in some of these conversations with executive directors of local social service organizations. Lucky Boothe of the City's Parks, Forestry & Recreation Department and Dixon Hall's Kenneth Slater convened many of these gatherings.

Although public and private foundations had been funding programs in the neighbourhood for decades, it became very clear that no one was talking to each other. For the most part, local agencies were competing against each other for scarce philanthropic dollars, rather than coordinating and collaborating on proposals to the funding bodies.

There had to be a better way. In response, we proposed a "collective impact fund" to a large group of charitable foundations in 2013. It was one of those big boardroom presentations, with everyone nodding and listening intently and then politely thanking us for the proposal. Our pitch fell on deaf ears.

We went at it a second time in February 2017, shortly after Daniele Zanotti had taken the reins at United Way Greater Toronto. This time around, we brought a $250,000 pledge to the table to kick-start the fund.

Zanotti embraced the concept immediately and brought other funders to the table. Hand in hand with local residents, social service agencies, TCH, Daniels, and the City of Toronto, Zanotti's team, led by Ruth Crammond and Nation Cheong, shaped a participatory grant-making process.

Maple Leaf Sports & Entertainment led the way at the Athletic Grounds. United Way picked up the ball and ran farther down the field. Participatory grant-making is messy and challenging, but the good news is that all stakeholders are now talking to each other and strategic social infrastructure investments are being made.

A participant at Dixon Hall's Mill Centre hones their carpentry skills under the guidance of professional instructors.

The other good news is that Zanotti and Darryl White, CEO of Bank of Montreal, have leveraged lessons learned from Regent Park and other priority neighbourhoods to create a cross-sectoral approach to building inclusive, resilient communities. The Inclusive Local Economic Opportunity initiative, aka ILEO, is bringing all sectors together to reduce gaps in economic prosperity at the neighbourhood level.

Zanotti and White kicked off the process by bringing twenty influential CEOs to the same table with community stakeholders from Scarborough's Golden Mile neighbourhood. This powerful cross-sectoral team is making a significant impact, with ILEO pilot projects underway well before the first shovel hits the ground on a twenty-five-year transformation of the Golden Mile neighbourhood.

The ILEO model is replicable across the city and beyond, a made-in-Toronto approach to building strong, inclusive communities through partnership and collaboration.

BRIDGE
Creating a Social Infrastructure Investment Fund

Presented to Daniele Zanotti, CEO, United Way Greater Toronto, February 2017

Toronto Community Housing, working closely with residents and other neighbourhood stakeholders, established a framework within which the Regent Park revitalization is unfolding.

A comprehensive zoning bylaw is guiding the development of roads, sewers, and buildings, and a Social Development Plan (SDP) is guiding the development of the social infrastructure.

The Regent Park revitalization is moving forward with great momentum. New roads are reconnecting the neighbourhood to the rest of the city. New rental buildings are providing a new perspective and optimism for over two thousand families that have lived in homes that are barely fit for habitation.

Although the revitalization is moving in the right direction, many significant challenges remain. To many in the broader city, all the shiny new buildings signify that Regent Park has been "fixed," that the past has been erased.

On the ground in the community, however, it is very clear that much more needs to be done. Decades of poverty, combined with physical and emotional isolation, has resulted in significant alienation from the broader community, particularly among young Regent Park residents.

The overall challenge of the revitalization is to ensure that the social infrastructure will be as strong as the physical, that the initial seeds of social cohesion that were planted will not only survive but flourish.

Although funding is in place for the first three phases of physical infrastructure, there is *no* funding available to nurture and support the creation of a healthy social infrastructure. Given current fiscal realities, it is highly unlikely that governments at any level will be making the investment required to ensure success beyond the bricks and mortar.

As such, new partners need to be brought to the table, and a new paradigm of philanthropy developed to reflect the realities of a revitalization, which, by its very nature, unfolds over a long period of time.

A number of charitable foundations have extensive histories of supporting worthwhile programs and agencies within Regent Park. Many continue to support specific projects and are inundated with requests for additional support.

The opportunity today is move away from a one-off approach to a more strategic and longer-term approach through development of the Regent Park Social Infrastructure Investment Fund.

The next five years are critical, and strategic investments need to be made to ensure the goals of the SDP will be realized.

This fund is an opportunity to create a long-term partnership between the philanthropic sector and the Regent Park revitalization, a mechanism by which strategic investments reinforce each other, like steel within concrete, to ensure a strong social infrastructure for the "new" Regent Park.

VERSE THIRTY-SIX

AN AFFORDABLE AND ACCESSIBLE COMMUNITY

THERE IS a lot of talk in "city-building" circles about inclusion, but with no clarity on what it means or what it looks like on the ground. One aspect of inclusion is to integrate homes for people of all ages within new communities. Older people add wisdom, depth, and texture, bringing opportunities for inter-generational exchange that enhance lived experiences for everyone. Residents of the Sumach by Chartwell are bringing their life skills and energy to the table, adding value through every interchange with both young and older residents throughout the community.

A further fundamental building block is actively addressing income disparity. How do we close the gap? What tools can be leveraged in order to build communities in which everyone has an opportunity to learn, grow, work, and prosper?

Social procurement programs, along with workforce development collaborations with TCH, Yonge Street Mission, Pathways to Education,

Dixon Hall, George Brown College, and University of Toronto have made an impact. Jobs and career path opportunities have been created for hundreds of local residents.

However, closing the income disparity gap is only one part of the equation. Inclusive communities must also integrate both affordable rental and ownership opportunities. An inclusive community must also go well beyond minimum requirements of the building code to ensure accessibility.

AFFORDABILITY

We pushed the affordability envelope as far as it could be pushed. At the outset, there were 2,083 deeply affordable homes within the sixty-nine-acre community, with affordability enshrined through a federal program under which tenants pay rent geared to income (RGI).

Although those subsidies will be replaced, RGI homes will represent approximately 25 percent of the overall unit count on completion. Seventy-five percent will be sold or leased at market value, with a small percentage at a more affordable rental rate, slightly below market.

Some planners and urbanists will celebrate the 75:25 ratio as representative of most neighbourhoods in Toronto. Others will lament that the process should have resulted in a higher affordability percentage.

Regardless of the ultimate ratio, we saw the revitalization as an opportunity for TCH to devolve ownership of its new buildings to non-profit co-ops, rather than maintaining ownership within an unwieldy 58,000-unit portfolio. Unfortunately, we were consistently told to keep our hands and ideas off the merchandise. Although that bird failed to fly, we pushed to increase the overall number of affordable units, as well as to integrate affordable units within market buildings and townhome blocks. In fact, I used half of a bottle of Wite-Out drawing and redrawing groups of townhomes in Phase Two, demonstrating how tenants in TCH townhomes could live side by side with owners of market townhomes. On several occasions, we also offered TCH opportunities to own suites integrated within condominium buildings. On each occasion, management at the housing company said, "Thanks, but no thanks."

Unable to make some of the big moves toward integration, we worked with TCH to create several pathways to affordable homeownership. The Foundation Program, for example, is a down payment assistance program implemented in partnership with TCH and the City of Toronto. Seventeen TCH tenants became homeowners with shared equity second mortgages up to 35 percent of the purchase price. BOOST, a second affordable ownership initiative, provided a hand up to home ownership to 211 first-time buyers from Regent Park and across the city with a 10 percent second mortgage.

Both Foundation and BOOST utilized small pools of residual capital from a federal and provincial contribution agreement with the City of Toronto. Sean Gadon, the City of Toronto's entrepreneurial affordable housing guru at the time, brought these funds to the table. However, when they were gone, they were gone.

In response, we stepped in with a $5 million commitment to create the Partnership for Affordable Homeownership (PAH) in Phase Three, a shared equity second mortgage program offering up to 50 percent of the purchase price exclusively to Regent Park residents. Ten households will achieve homeownership through this initiative, and each will contribute one hundred hours of volunteer work in the community prior to move-in, further embedding each participant in the life of the community.

Small in number but powerful in impact, three additional households became homeowners within Regent Park through our long-standing partnership with Habitat for Humanity GTA, and two more Habitat partner families are scheduled to move into our next condominium in 2025. Ene Underwood, Habitat GTA's executive director, has made an enormous impact across the city, and there is no better moment than sharing a "key ceremony" with Ene and a partner family as they are handed the key to their new home.

Martin Blake also teamed up with Gadon to create a groundbreaking affordable rental program.

Partnership for Affordable Living (PAL) is a program by which deeply affordable rental homes are seamlessly integrated within purpose-built market rental buildings. EVOLV, a market rental building in Phase Three developed in partnership with Sun Life Financial, is the highly successful test bed for this cross-sectoral demonstration.

Blake and Gadon, together with WoodGreen Community Services, connected all the dots to create a beautiful composition. The City of Toronto brought $5.1 million to the table, enabling WoodGreen, the non-profit partner, to enter a forty-year head lease with the private sector partners—Daniels and Sun Life.

Today, thirty-four graduates of WoodGreen's Homeward Bound program are paying rents significantly below market within a market rental building, a brilliant demonstration of what can be achieved when all sectors come together to create both affordability and integration.

ACCESSIBILITY

Accessibility is another essential ingredient of an inclusive community. The bad news is that the building code is the lowest common denominator when it comes to building homes and communities that are truly accessible. The good news is that a movement that took flight in Regent Park is making significant strides to change the dial on accessibility across the country.

Flash back to 2016 when Jake Cohen received feedback from homeowners about accessibility challenges within their suites and common areas. Recognizing the disconnect between what the code requires and what would make a building truly accessible, Jake and Brock Stevenson, of our team, engaged Quadrangle Architects to step up our deliverables on accessibility. In turn, accessible design advocate Lorene Casiez of Quadrangle (now BDP Quadrangle) introduced us to Luke Anderson of StopGap Foundation, known for creating colorful ramps to facilitate accessibility to retail storefronts.

Jake and Brock invited Luke on "roll-through" evaluations in two of our recently completed condominium buildings. Luke, a powerful advocate in the accessibility community, gave us the straight goods. In short: even in code-certified "barrier-free" suites, a person in a wheelchair couldn't access their balcony or roll into the shower in their home. Many of our common amenity areas were also not accessible.

Those initial conversations led to the implementation of our Accessibility Design Program (ADP), which includes significantly enhanced design standards that Brock, Marco Chow, and other team members are incorporating in new builds across our portfolio. Brock and Marco are also working closely with Rick Hansen Foundation, embracing their expertise and advice to ensure our new buildings achieve Rick Hansen Gold, their highest certification level.

Immediate interest in ADP came from L'Arche Toronto, an organization serving individuals with intellectual disabilities. Jake nurtured that relationship, and ultimately, we co-created River House with Raphael Arens and the L'Arche team, an eight-bedroom unit in our Artworks condominiums at Dundas and River Streets. River House is a living, breathing testament to inclusion, a demonstration of what can be achieved through cross-sectoral collaboration.

Jake, Megan Aird, and other members of the Daniels team also engaged Maayan Ziv and her team from AccessNow to conduct a Regent Park "Map Mission," identifying what we had done well and where we had totally missed the mark on accessibility.

Luke's feedback, lessons learned from River House, and AccessNow's Map Mission were total eye-openers. We had to do better, so we set out to engage our industry and the accessibility community by creating the Accelerating Accessibility Coalition (AAC). Although it is still in its infancy, significant progress is being made. Developers, builders, designers, and architects, along with StopGap, AccessNow, Rick Hansen Foundation, Older Women's Network, Sunnybrook Hospital, Seneca College, the University of Toronto, and others have coalesced under the AAC banner, spearheaded by the unstoppable Linda Weichel and ULI Toronto's Richard Joy.

Together, we will build a more inclusive world. Affordable. Accessible. And with a constant effort to close the income disparity gap to ensure that everyone will be welcome in all our communities.

Sakina (far left) and members of the sewing circle create the first commissioned quilt, which now hangs in the lobby of Paintbox Condominiums.

VERSE THIRTY-SEVEN

THE REVELATION OF SOCIAL PROCUREMENT

MEETING SAKINA KHANAM holds a special place in my archive of memorable moments.

A chance encounter on Dundas Street inspired an approach to social procurement that has resonated within our company and will ideally become standard operating procedure throughout the development industry.

In that first conversation on Dundas, Sakina lamented that many families in the community weren't able to bring money into their households. She reflected on life back home in Bangladesh, where women often bartered their sewing products and handmade quilts for food, clothes, and services.

In that moment, a switch went from off to on, shining a light on a new way to think about impactful community investment.

With that light shining brightly, Heela and I visited Sakina and several friends from the neighbourhood in their windowless studio in a TCH building slated for demolition. Not only did we look at photographs that became the inspiration for our first commissioned quilt, but also we were honoured with a full meal featuring the most delicious chicken biryani ever.

In subsequent weeks, Heela, along with Manal Siddiqui, a community-minded young woman, mentored Sakina's sewing circle through the business proposition of creating and selling an original piece of art. The quilt, called *Regent Park—A Love Poem*, was ultimately commissioned and designed to hang behind the concierge desk at Paintbox Condominiums, our first condominium building in Phase Two.

Unveiling the quilt was truly a memorable moment, with new condo owners meeting each other and the Bengali women who had created a monumentally beautiful work of art for their lobby. There wasn't a dry eye in the house as Sakina spoke about the challenges they faced, as well as the joy of being able to welcome new residents to Regent Park and to share her community's art with all of them.

Today, quilts by Sakina's sewing circle hang proudly in buildings throughout Regent Park, and the lessons learned from that experience continue to shape our trajectory as a company.

Shortly after that initial revelation on Dundas, I met Iftikhar Uddin Ahmed at an event in the neighbourhood. After showing me his resumé, which featured awards and gallery shows around the world, Iftikhar told me that it had been impossible to mount a show in Toronto.

I visited his apartment a few days later and was blown away by his work. Most impactful was seeing the large number of paintings racked and stacked within every closet. In Ifthikar's words, these paintings would likely "never see the light of day."

That moment led to the opening of the Regent Park Rotating Gallery in the Presentation Centre, which has presented Iftikhar's work and the work of many other local artists over the past seven years.

Fast-forward to May 4, 2018, a memorable day at Daniels Spectrum and an exhibition we sponsored by Yasin Osman called *Dear Ayeeyo*. Yasin had been making a positive impact in Regent Park for many years through Shoot for Peace, a grassroots mentorship program that engages young people in storytelling through photography.

On that day, Yasin was opening his first solo exhibition, a collection of intimate scenes and portraits from everyday life within villages of Somalia, his parents' homeland. Yasin's portraits showed the world a different side of the humanitarian crisis in Somalia, one filled with hope and love.

I arrived just before Yasin's remarks to several thousand Somali guests from across Southern Ontario, many of whom had come to Canada under duress and faced many challenges on their journey to this country. That evening, however, they were celebrating one of their own. The pride, joy, and spirit of community were deeply moving.

BRIDGE
"Quilt of Love"

R*egent Park—A Love Poem*, our first quilt, now hanging in the lobby of Paintbox Condominiums, inspired one of the most powerful moments within *The Journey Musical*. "Quilt of Love" was performed by Charlotte Siegel, a young woman who grew from the classrooms of the Regent Park School of Music to the big stage as a member of the Canadian Opera Company.

"QUILT OF LOVE" from *The Journey Musical*

One time, they were lost, random pieces all around, pictures of
    our history laid out on the ground.
Now they are your poem, this wondrous tapestry, the stories of our
    neighbourhood displayed for all to see.

There's me in the playground, swinging high and free, safe within
    the comfort, of you watching over me.
There's you on the park bench beneath the big old tree, cut down
    with a promise, a better home for you and me.

And now you lift us up, with your quilt of love. When you lift us up,
    you bring us harmony.

You drew a pattern with stories from our past, sewing squares of fabric,
    that make the memories last.
You stitched it all together, working day and night, so we could live in the light...
    so we could live in the light.

There's the little garden, watered with your tears, where you prayed
    for peace and safety, nothing left to fear.
Now we have your poem of love, displayed beside the door, proudly there
    for all to see, sad hands nevermore.

Now you lift us up with your quilt of love. When you lift us up,
    you bring us harmony.

VERSE THIRTY-EIGHT

COMING OF AGE: THE WORLD URBAN PAVILION

O UR THREE ORGANIZING elements have stood the test of time: food and urban agriculture, active sports and recreation, and arts and culture. Each one flows, grows, and intersects with a myriad of melodies, all fuelling the overall mission... building a healthy, resilient social infrastructure.

Like a jazz solo, a revitalization is never a straight line, but rather a series of twists and turns with a complex web of relationships to navigate.

Although the public/private partnership model is fundamental to success, it is a daunting challenge, particularly when the public-sector partner is susceptible to shifting political winds.

The bottom line is that TCH's governance structure is problematic. Imagine trying to run a company that owns 58,000 social housing units, all in need of major repair. And then imagine the company has only one shareholder, one susceptible to a four-year election cycle, doling out decision making to a board with time-limited authority.

Within the umbrella of those challenges, TCH's teams on the ground have done great work. Often constrained by political and economic handcuffs, each successive team has been deeply committed to the mission. Liz Root, Annely Zonena, Lizette Zuniga, Tom Burr, Heather Grey-Wolf, Leslie Gash, Ilidio Coito, Vincent Tong, Kelly Skeith, Abigail Moriah, Jed Kilbourn, Jessica Hawes, Peter Zimmerman, Mirej Vasic, Sean Major, Tereza Todorova, William Mendes, Shane Bourne, and many others have put heart and soul into making it all work, as have TCH hall of famers Barry Thomas, Lancefield Morgan, and Julio Rigores.

Despite shifting political winds and endless predictions of doom, three phases and fifty-four acres are nearing completion, with abundant evidence that the revitalization is working. A key testament to its effectiveness came when UN-Habitat, Canada Mortgage and Housing Corporation (CMHC), and the Urban Economy Forum (UEF) chose Regent Park for their World Urban Pavilion.

It all started with a phone call from Simona, our VP of marketing and communications, imploring me to take an interview with *Bloomberg News*. Simona knows that I prefer Jake, Martin, Heela, or Remo to be front and centre on media opportunities. However, when she twists my arm to do an interview, it's for a good reason. In this case, Natalie Wong was intent on interviewing me, and with Simona's urging, I agreed.

Bloomberg News published Wong's story on August 6, 2019, under the headline "A Toronto Builder Fights Housing Price Crisis (He Also Writes Songs)." The story caught the attention of folks at UN-Habitat in Nairobi, who alerted colleagues in Mexico City, who asked colleagues at the UEF in Toronto to check out what had been happening.

UEF reached out, and our social impact team, Fatima Saya and Heela Omarkhail, hosted a walkabout with Reza Pourvaziry and a few colleagues. Fatima and Heela blew their socks off, which led to Pourvaziry inviting Heela and I to share the keynote podium at UEF's inaugural forum on October 28 and 29, 2019.

Heela inspired delegates with stories about social infrastructure initiatives underway within the revitalization. I spent my podium time outlining an opportunity to create a global knowledge exchange hub that would project best practices in building healthy, resilient communities around the world.

In closing, we invited everyone to join us on a Regent Park walkabout the following evening.

VERSE THIRTY-NINE

AN IMPACTFUL WALKABOUT

THE WALKABOUT on October 29, 2019, was pure magic. Thirty-five delegates from around the world gathered around the scale model in the Presentation Centre, the best place to get a feel for the scale of a sixty-nine-acre revitalization.

The sun was setting on a spectacular fall evening as Heela, Fatima, and I set out with our guests to walk around the community. The first stop is always the corner of Regent and Cole Streets in Phase One, otherwise known as Guessing Game Corner. Which buildings are condo? Which are rental, owned by TCH? And that, of course, is the whole point—for most observers, it's impossible to tell.

The big park was full of life: kids on swings; families out for a walk; dogs running free in the off-leash park, with their owners comparing doggie notes; gardeners working in the community gardens beside the bake oven.

As we walked by the Pam McConnell Aquatic Centre, everyone wondered why we couldn't see the pools. The answer blew their minds: the blinds were drawn because this was one of several time slots when Muslim women enjoy a private women-only swim, a brilliant recognition of the cultural diversity of the community.

From the Aquatic Centre, we crossed Dundas Street and continued south to the Athletic Grounds, a sight that always stirs my soul. From Wite-Out scribbles on a site plan to something very special.

The exterior lights had just come on, reflecting a soft twilight on our faces. Two half-field soccer games were underway; weight-lifters were lifting; the basketball court was teeming with people of all ages. Runners were running, and a group of kids were comparing cartwheel skills beside the track.

Best of all, we bumped into Regent Park residents Hannah (aka my daughter) and Mr. Eko, her wonderful Frenchie, on their evening stroll around the Athletic Grounds.

On our way to Daniels Spectrum, we were waylaid at F/X, George Brown College's (GBC) Fashion Exchange. Something fun was happening there. I peeked in to find GBC's then president, Anne Sado, hosting a party in celebration of Hewlett-Packard's donation of state-of-the-art digital pattern making and cutting equipment. Although the party was in full swing, President Sado invited us in for a glass of champagne and an impromptu presentation on the powerful role that post-secondary institutions can play as active partners in community.

And then, once we had continued from there, we had a truly OMG moment: we walked into Daniels Spectrum and were met by a group of twelve-foot-tall circus artists. No, they weren't really twelve feet tall; they were on stilts preparing for a show in support of Square Circle, a non-profit Social Circus arts organization, founded by Clarence Ford. Regent Park was blessed when Ford, an award-winning choreographer, artistic director, and producer, brought Square Circle to Daniels Spectrum in 2013.

The final bit of serendipity was a chance encounter with Farid Jalil, a key member of Artscape's management team at the Spectrum. Farid is a master storyteller, and over the years his stories have informed and inspired songs in *The Journey Musical*. Although he was heading for home, Farid shared his story of growing up in the community. That evening, his words brought many of us to tears, and it didn't take long for the experience of the walkabout to sink in for the folks from UN-Habitat and UEF.

VERSE FORTY

A BRILLIANT OUTCOME

THE NEXT MORNING, Pourvaziry from UEF called to express a desire to create a global knowledge exchange hub in Regent Park.

Fast-forward to April 21, 2022, opening day of the World Urban Pavilion in Regent Park—Powered by Daniels, a collaboration between UN-Habitat, CMHC, UEF, and The Daniels Corporation. This was a true coming-of-age moment for the community, being selected as the platform from which best practices in city-building would be projected around the world.

Many people pitched in to make that happen, but key among them was Ana Bailão from the City of Toronto, Courtney Glen from Mayor Tory's office, Minister of International Development Ahmed Hussen from the federal government, and Romy Bowers, Debbie Stewart, and Steffan Jones at CMHC.

Matti Siemiatycki and Lara Muldoon of the University of Toronto's School of Cities kick-started programming at the Pavilion, followed by programs presented by former dean Richard Sommer and his team from the John H. Daniels Faculty of Architecture, Landscape, and Design.

Over the first two years, thousands of people from around the world participated in programs delivered by co-chairs Reza Pourvaziry and Eduardo López Moreno, along with Acting Deputy Director Alex Venuto, Fazileh Dadvar-Khani, Ilda Cordeiro, and the World Urban Pavilion team.

Most importantly, a group of local residents, including Marlene DeGenova, Walied Khogali, Ismail Afrah, Deany Peters, Gail Lynch, Ines Garcia, Miguel Avila-Velarde, Ibrahim Afrah, and Sureya Ibrahim, ensured that the Regent Park story is properly projected from the Pavilion to the world.

It didn't take long for the broader world to take note of the transformation. In fact, the Regent Park story caught the attention of the World Economic Forum (WEF), and in October 2023, WEF presented TCH and Daniels with a Public-Private Partnership Award recognizing Regent Park as a model for urban transformation internationally.

VERSE FORTY-ONE

AN ENCORE WITH INFINITE POSSIBILITIES

R**EGENT PARK** is no longer a food desert or a place to avoid. It is no longer a community consisting entirely of social housing, disconnected from the world beyond its footprint.

In fact, the entire city is connecting with Regent Park, swimming at the Aquatic Centre, enjoying Taste of Regent Park, playing soccer at the Athletic Grounds, watching films under the stars with the Regent Park Film Festival, and experiencing Indigenous theatre with Native Earth Performing Arts.

Today, Benny Bing, Komi Olaf, Melissa Falconer, and Morgan-Paige Melbourne are bringing the "living lane" to life, creating both art and community from their work/live spaces, while Iftikhar Uddin Ahmed, Gabrielle Lasporte, Mazhar (Muhammad Muzharul Haque), Yasin Osman, and other local artists are building their portfolios and practices.

Dixon Hall Music School and Community Music Schools of Toronto (formerly Regent Park School of Music) welcome hundreds of young people to their classes. Most will build both personal and musical skills.

A few will grow into the next Thompson Egbo-Egbo, one of Canada's greatest jazz pianists, or Charlotte Siegel, the brightest new star at the Canadian Opera Company.

Walking the streets today, we feel the impact of collective effort, of a large ensemble of people and personalities adding tones and texture within every bar of the composition. Building community is very much like playing music: jamming with eyes and ears wide open, listening deeply and being generous with every player, building bridges and friendships through every refrain.

And as the revitalization continues to unfold, new people and new instruments will join the ensemble, with unlimited potential to create new harmonies, stories, and songs. Although our contractual relationship with Toronto Community Housing will come to an end, the Daniels team will continue to be there, adding value where we can.

And of course, I'll be there as well, for years to come... walking the streets, having coffee at Café ZUZU, a croissant at Le Beau, or just hanging out at Daniels Spectrum, listening carefully as the rhythms of change continue to energize and inspire, with great hope for the future.

OUTRO

THE WORLD'S URBAN POPULATION is projected to increase by 68 percent by 2050. With that reality in front of us, cities must find ways to accommodate the need for enhanced infrastructure, basic services, and housing, as well as employment and leisure opportunities.

As the population grows, climate change and environmental hazards will amplify inequalities and increase the vulnerability of a significant percentage of the world's population. Conflicts and migration dynamics will further increase vulnerability within urban populations.

Spatial inequality is significantly higher in 75 percent of the world's cities compared to two decades ago, and the resulting fragmentation is manifesting itself as segregation, with a concentration of poverty in certain areas of the cities.

The Regent Park story illustrates how to push back on these trends, and *Rhythms of Change* clearly demonstrates both the value and complexity of urban regeneration processes. As communities around the world engage with municipal authorities and businesses to achieve transformative results, Regent Park provides an exceptional road map.

As a forgotten and ill-conceived path in the history of a young city, Regent Park had been left to decay, with a crowd of buildings standing as silent witness to an urban shipwreck. Over time, with local residents at centre stage, the stars aligned in favour of positive change. Institutional initiatives found each other, individual willpower came together, and innovative ideas amalgamated within an urban design and social transformation process.

In short, everything connected in a clear sequence, resulting in substantive change to the urban fabric.

Mitchell Cohen's narrative is a testimonial to a new and fresh approach, a cross-sectoral collaboration resulting in vibrant streets and parks full of people and joy. Regent Park is a giant living monument to how transformation can integrate and respect local residents and the history of a community, a revolutionary urban regeneration recognized throughout the world. New partnerships and models of development were rooted in the idea of dignity. Communal areas, meeting places, recreational facilities, and well-designed social housing allow residents to get to know each other, recognize themselves in their intrinsic differences and similitudes, enabling the formation of a new identity and sense of belonging.

When building on local assets and strong participatory processes, urban regeneration strengthens a sense of identity and enriches diversity. By engaging the expertise, resources, and innovation of the private sector, more vibrant, equitable, and sustainable communities can be created.

Urban regeneration represents a worldwide priority to "localize" sustainable development goals (SDGs) established by the United Nations in 2015. Regeneration is also recognized as one of the most effective processes to promote spatial inclusion and climate action while creating more inclusive, resilient, safe, and sustainable cities.

By increasing density in neighbourhoods, generating value through intensification, and leveraging that value by engaging the private sector, we can create more compact, walkable, and connected communities that promote social equity, reduce income segregation, and enhance urban livability.

The revitalization of Regent Park is doing all of that, demonstrating a human-centric and integrated approach, honouring a historical working class and new migrants in search of a better life.

A seed of light, a few drops of water, a tomorrow that could be reborn and replicated around the world, a footprint that never ends. Those footprints are already making their mark in communities around the world, with each specific context reflecting unique local characteristics and challenges. However, some very clear common principles are emerging.

Urban revitalization requires collaboration and partnership with local organizations, businesses, and government agencies. Placing people at the centre is key to mitigate and manage risks. To make a positive impact, it is important to listen deeply to local voices, engaging and involving residents in every stage of the process. Not lip service. Deep engagement.

There is much to learn from the Regent Park story. *Rhythms of Change* illuminates a path forward, portraying perseverance, ingenuity, and the human agency that wants to change things and knows how to do it.

If you represent a government or public institution, private sector, community or research group, university, or any other interested urban actor, apply the lessons you've learned from this book within the context of your community. And then reinforce your global presence by sharing the experiences and best practices from your initiatives. While each initiative is unique, let us all join forces to co-develop knowledge products, create more impact, and mobilize all relevant stakeholders to generate better value together.

    Join us in shaping a future of inclusive and sustainable urban regeneration, nurturing a network that thrives on collaboration, learning, and a shared commitment to making our cities better places for everyone.

Rafael Tuts, director, Global Solutions Division,
United Nations Human Settlements Programme, UN-Habitat

Eduardo López Moreno, co-chair, Urban Economy Forum,
former director at Habitat Office Mexico and Cuba, and
head of Knowledge and Innovation at UN-Habitat in Nairobi, Kenya

CODA

With the final grace notes of narrative complete, the following provides a by-the-numbers summary, including information on the stellar lineup of architectural firms that have contributed to the fabric of the community.

SUMMARY OF PHASES ONE, TWO, AND THREE

Completed or under construction: 4,345 market units, composed of
- 3,058 market condominiums completed and 643 under construction,
- 312 market rental suites completed, and
- 332 market seniors' suites completed.

An additional 280 market units and 56 affordable units are in development.

In addition, 34 affordable rental units have been incorporated into market buildings by Daniels.

TCHC units completed or under construction: 1,462, composed of
- 925 RGI TCHC replacement units completed, 189 under construction, and
- 300 affordable rental TCHC units completed, 24 under construction.

A total of 242,000 square feet of commercial and retail space has been completed or is under construction.

PHASE ONE

418 TCHC units were demolished in Phase One, replaced by 520 market condominiums and 365 TCHC rental units.

Block 11: TCHC Rental
84 units
Design architect: Kearns Mancini Architects
Architect of record (AoR):
Graziani + Corazza Architects

Block 12: One Park West Condominiums
176 units
Architect: CORE Architects

Block 13: One Cole Condominiums
293 units
Design architect: Diamond Schmitt Architects
AoR: Graziani + Corazza Architects

Block 14: TCHC Rental
224 units
Design architect: architects-Alliance
AoR: Graziani + Corazza Architects

Blocks 11 & 12: Market Townhomes
51 units
Architect: Graziani + Corazza Architects

Blocks 12 & 14: TCHC Rental Townhomes
29 units
Architect: Graziani + Corazza Architects

30 Regent Street: TCHC Rental Townhomes
28 units
Architect: Graziani + Corazza Architects

Block 14—M1: Market Project (in development)
336 units, including 280 market units
and 56 affordable units
Architect: Diamond Schmitt Architects

Rendering in progress

PHASE TWO

499 TCHC units were demolished in Phase Two, replaced by 1,270 market condominiums and 428 TCHC rental units.

Block 20: TCHC Rental
155 units
Architect: Wallman Architects

Block 21: Bartholomew Condominiums & Townhomes
189 units
Architect: Quadrangle Architects Limited
(now BDP Quadrangle)

Block 22: TCHC Rental
118 units (86 midrise and 32 townhomes)
Architect: Giannone Petricone Associates

239

Block 23: The Sutton Collection
18 condominium townhomes and
semi-detached homes
Architect: KIRKOR Architects and Planners

Block 24 North: Paintbox Condominiums
282 units
Architect: Diamond Schmitt Architects

Block 24 North: Daniels Spectrum
60,000-square-foot community cultural hub
Architect: Diamond Schmitt Architects

Block 24 South: TCHC Rental
155 units
Architect: Diamond Schmitt Architects

Block 25: One Park Place North & South Towers
781 units
Architect: Hariri Pontarini Architects

PHASE THREE

654 TCHC units were demolished in Phase Three, replaced by a total of 3,258 units, including 1,911 market condominiums, 346 purpose-built rental units (EVOLV), 332 market seniors' units (Sumach by Chartwell), and 669 TCHC rental units.

Block 1: Daniels on Parliament North & South Towers Condominiums (under construction)
643 units
Design architect: Superkül
AoR: KIRKOR Architects and Planners

Block 16 North: TCHC Rental
213 units
Design architect: RAW Design
AoR: Rafael + Bigauskas Architects

Block 16 South: DuEast & DuEast Boutique Condominiums
435 units
Architect: CORE Architects

Block 17 North: TCHC Rental
158 units
Architect: Wallman Architects

Block 17 South: Artworks Tower &
Artsy Boutique Condominiums
465 units
Design architect: BDP Quadrangle
AoR: KIRKOR Architects and Planners

Block 26: The Wyatt Condominiums
344 units
Design architect: KPMB Architects
AoR: Page Steele Architects and Arcadis IBI Group

Block 27: TCHC Rental
276 units
Architect: RAW Design

Block 28: TCHC Rental Townhomes
22 units
Architect: Van Elslander + Associates Architects

Block 30: EVOLV Rentals
346 units, including 312 market rental and 34 affordable rental units
Architect: Arcadis IBI Group

Block 30: Field House Townhomes
24 condominium townhomes
Architect: Arcadis IBI Group

Block 32: The Sumach by Chartwell
332 seniors' apartments
Architect: SvN Architects + Planners

LINER NOTES

Janice: You are the best listener I've ever met. Your wisdom and insightful feedback helped me navigate endless challenges in real time, as well as in the retelling within this book.

Hannah and Jake: Our kids, who have inspired me to do everything I can to make the world a better place. It is incredibly fun and deeply rewarding to be your father.

Hannah: It has been a revelation as Mr. Eko has brought out the hidden dog lover in me. It is always a tremendous pleasure to visit your home in Regent Park and walk the neighbourhood with you and Mr. Eko.

Jake: It is so exciting to witness your evolution as the leader of our company. It is also wonderful to be immersed in family life with you and Lisa and our two incredible grandkids, Jack and Mia, whose boundless energy reinforces my desire to keep firing on all cylinders.

I will be forever grateful to my mentor, friend, and partner, John Daniels. "Jack" gave me the keys to a kingdom of opportunity, and we have built our company on the foundation of his mantra—to always "do the right thing."

Tom Dutton and Jim Aird took that mantra on the road with me and co-created the company we have become.

Martin Blake was the calm in the eye of the storm, our steady-handed leader and guide through the challenges of a public/private partnership. Martin's steel-trap memory was incredibly helpful in reconstructing some of the most memorable moments as these "reflections" took shape.

Heela Omarkhail has risen to every challenge and opportunity, making a significant positive impact within Regent Park and across our entire portfolio. Heela inspires me and everyone she meets. Fatima Saya built strong relationships in the community from the moment she joined our team. Heela and Fatima provided detailed feedback and fact-checking to ensure these reflections are as accurate as possible.

Simona Annibale has been at the heart of building our company for over twenty-five years. Simona was a receptionist in our Richmond Hill sales office when we met. At age eighteen, she gave me the straight goods that day and has done so ever since, shaping the trajectory of our company, as well as the shape and creative content of this book.

Gabriella Breault's diligent work gathering photographs and Daron Blackburn's and Megan Aird's creativity and dedication were instrumental in putting the book together and building awareness for its release. The entire Daniels marketing and communications team ensures that all our stories are told with both passion and humility.

Dominic Tompa, Tiffany Wood, Caroline Mosby, Linda Fa, Genny Liu-Thomas, and the Daniels Realty team have told the Regent Park story to thousands of people over the years, and over three thousand have made the decision to purchase a home, becoming part of the evolution of this remarkable community.

Despite leasing up within the challenges of COVID-19, Adam Molson and our Gateway leasing team brought EVOLV to life, establishing a new benchmark for urban rental living, integrating affordable suites into the fabric of the best rental asset in the city. Stephen Clifford and Steven Kiss were stellar in the lease-up phase, and Kelsey McKibbon, of our impact team, and Izabela Konopka, our property manager, have created engaging activations, generating a powerful spirit of community that flows from within the building into the broader neighbourhood.

Don Pugh, Nicole Ferrari, Sasha Annibale, James Yaneff, and our commercial leasing team told the Regent Park story to potential commercial tenants and curated a mix of national brand and independent retail operators who bring goods, services, and vitality to street life within the community. Miles Jones brings the essence of cool to Regent Park just by living in the community, but his help landing 611 Purple Factory and Pro League Sports is also greatly appreciated.

Remo Agostino, Gokul Pisharoty, Steve Langdon, Antonella Spano, Ian Nastor, Andrew Marson, Brian Merkley, Rose Zonni, Sonya Smith, Joe Brindley, Alison Platt, Brock Stevenson, Mike Matunin, Duncan Smith, Ginette Battikha, Judy Lem, Carol Krasovskis, Niall Haggart, Sam Tassone, and many other members of the Daniels team sweated over the details through every twist and turn. It takes a very large family of dedicated and talented people to build a community.

Mark Guslits, John Fox, Sean Meagher, Tony Boston, John Gladki, Ken Greenberg, Greg Spearn, Sean Gadon, and Celia Smith have been pivotal players within the revitalization, and each has been wonderfully generous with feedback as I relived the stories of their roles within the evolution of the community.

Deany Peters, Diane MacLean, Debra Dineen, Ines Garcia, Gail Lynch, Marlene DeGenova, Yasin Osman, Richard Marsella, Adonis Huggins, Kenneth Slater, Lloyd Pike, Sureya Ibrahim, Ann Kirkland, Leonard

Schwartz, Alfred Jean-Baptiste, Trevlyn Kennedy, Angie Peters, Paulos Gebreyesus, Daniele Zanotti, and so many other friends who are living or working in the community have always spoken their minds, sharing their truths and shaping the course of our work.

Although she doesn't know it, Tracy Hanes, a *Toronto Star* contributor, inspired me to write this book. The headline of her article published in the *Star* on July 15th, 2023, asked "Hey, What Happened to Regent Park?" Although a lot had been written over the years, it felt that the time was right for me to help answer that question.

I started conceiving a few long-form magazine articles that would ideally be published in *Spacing* magazine. *Spacing*'s editor Dylan Reid was clear that the stories deserved to be told in book form. Thank you for that, Dylan... and for introducing me to Trena White and the team at Page Two Books, all of whom have been extraordinary collaborators in manifesting the stories in book form.

In particular, thank you to my editor, James Harbeck, for spending time with me in the community, listening carefully to the rhythms of change and helping shape my reflections into a coherent composition.

And finally, a heartfelt thank you to Henry Heillig, my musical mentor and songwriting partner. Your patience, guidance, and skill have enabled me to keep music at the heart of what I do. And for that I am forever grateful.

END NOTES

1. John Barber, "Condo Cash Was Going to Save Regent Park. Kiss That Idea (and Others) Goodbye," *Globe and Mail*, October 4, 2008, theglobeandmail.com/news/national/condo-cash-was-going-to-save-regent-park-kiss-that-idea-and-others-goodbye/article17972149.

2. Tristan Hopper, "Ex-Judge Called to Investigate Allegations against TCHC," *National Post*, March 12, 2012, nationalpost.com/posted-toronto/ex-judge-called-to-investigate-allegations-against-tchc.

3. Justin Skinner, "Regent Park Residents Defend Their Community at Rally," Toronto.com, April 4, 2012, toronto.com/news/regent-park-residents-defend-their-community-at-rally/article_383e19ef-188a-52d3-9db5-cfa5d0479fc9.html.

4. Excerpt from the LeSage report, August 2012. The report can be found at the end of this article: "TCHC Employees Didn't Break Rules During Purchases: Report," *CBC News*, August 10, 2012, cbc.ca/news/canada/toronto/tchc-employees-didn-t-break-rules-during-purchases-report-1.1185056.

PHOTO CREDITS

Gilad Cohen: p. ii
The Children's Book Bank: pp. x, 182–183
York University Libraries, Clara Thomas Archives & Special Collections: pp. 6
City of Toronto Archives: pp. 6, 23, 31
James Ip: pp. 7, 79, 82, 83, 100, 135, 154–155, 227
Nicola Betts: pp. 7 , 8, 11, 45, 135, 148
The Daniels Corporation: pp. 26, 86, 220, 237 (bottom), 241 (top), 245
Arthur Mola: pp. 36–37, 47, 48, 59, 63, 68–69, 83, 90–91, 110–111, 112, 131, 134, 137, 138–139, 140, 143, 144, 153, 156, 158, 162, 164–165, 192, 202, casewrap
Toronto Community Housing Corporation: pp. 42, 43, 56, 80, 92, 241 (middle)
torontocitylife.com: p. 43
Q&A Design: pp. 60–61
Ricky Ethier and Stephen Yu: p. 67
Agazi Afewerki: p. 71
Page Two: pp. 89, 117
Linda Edwards: p. 102
Rainer Soegtrop: p. 114
Paul Casselman: pp. 134, 168, 170, 184–185, 206, 216
Marni Grossman Photography: pp. 184, 237 (top & middle), 238–239, 240 (top two & bottom two), 241 (bottom), 242, 243 (top & middle), 244 (top)
Linda Stella: pp. 184, 185, 186, 191, 195
Photographer unknown: pp. 176–177, 240 (middle)
Phillip Gallard: p. 200
Yasin Osman: p. 229
Haseeb Khawaja: p. 243 (bottom)
Chartwell: p. 244 (bottom)
Alex Filipe: p. 252

ABOUT THE AUTHOR

MITCHELL COHEN is president and CEO of The Daniels Corporation, and has been steering the organization's strategic and long-term vision since 1984.

Under his leadership, Daniels has become known for building residential offerings for people at all stages of life, and for its commitment to building a healthy social infrastructure within each new community. Over the past four decades, the company has also created innovative, affordable rental programs as well as programs that help tenants become first-time homeowners.

Cohen has a master's in social psychology from the London School of Economics and a bachelor of science in psychology from McGill University. In 2019, Cohen was appointed to the Order of Canada in recognition of "his contributions to urban development and for his commitment to community building."

In 2013, he received an honorary doctorate from the Faculty of Community Services at Toronto Metropolitan University. In addition, Cohen has received the Queen Elizabeth II Diamond Jubilee Medal and an Award of Merit from the St. George's Society.

A songwriter and musician as well as a socially conscious real estate developer, Mitchell Cohen seamlessly bridges the intersection of business and the arts.

Copyright © 2024 by Mitchell Cohen

All rights reserved. No part of this book may be reproduced, stored in a retrieval system or transmitted, in any form or by any means, without the prior written consent of the publisher or a licence from The Canadian Copyright Licensing Agency (Access Copyright). For a copyright licence, visit accesscopyright.ca or call toll free to 1-800-893-5777.

Every reasonable effort has been made to contact and credit the copyright holders of images reproduced in this book. If you have any information regarding errors or omissions, please contact the publisher.

Cataloguing in publication information is available from Library and Archives Canada.

ISBN 978-1-77458-505-4 (hardcover)

Page Two
pagetwo.com

Edited by James Harbeck
Copyedited by Steph VanderMeulen
Book design by Jennifer Lum
Printed and bound in Canada by Friesens
Distributed in Canada by Raincoast Books
Distributed in the US and internationally by Macmillan

24 25 26 27 28   5 4 3 2 1

danielshomes.ca